the process of laying hold of them. Colleen Chao is a true encourager whose life and words exhort readers to take courage and worship Jesus with every breath.

LINDSEY CARLSON
Author of *A Better Encouragement: Trading Self-Help for True Hope*

Colleen's wealth of personal experience, biblical literacy, and knowledge of previous heroes of the Christian faith makes this devotional eminently accessible even while it broadens the reader's knowledge and love for the God of the ages. I commend it to Christians everywhere as a source of encouragement and joy, especially when the troubles of this life are pressing in and the time to cross that great river draws near.

BROOKS BUSER
President of Radius International

In the Hands of a Fiercely Tender God offers the truth about suffering. But Colleen doesn't leave us there—she gives us something tangible to hope in: Jesus. Through weaving stories from her own life, stories from saints of old, and solid biblical truths, Colleen gives us a beautiful tapestry of hope, through a series of daily devotionals. Whether in the thick darkness of suffering, or in the sunshine of ease—we all need these truths. This book makes me long to know Jesus more. What a gift!

KAREN RACE MCCUTCHEON
Former Special Assistant to the President and Director of White House Personnel, The White House (President George W. Bush); wife to a US diplomat

Praise for *In the Hands of a Fiercely Tender God*

Brave and bighearted, this book is like a series of coffee dates with a much-beloved friend. Colleen generously invites us to journey alongside her, not only through our suffering, but also into the joyous embrace of a Love that exceeds our wildest dreams. Every moment I spend with Colleen—in person and in print alike—leaves me more deeply convinced of the beauty of Jesus.

GREGORY COLES
Author of *No Longer Strangers: Finding Belonging in a World of Alienation*

With aching beauty, Colleen Chao beckons us to the deep waters, where we can behold our trials, sufferings, and hardships anew—as *In the Hands of a Fiercely Tender God*. Her writing, breathtaking and forged through the fire, will move you to tears and praise as she unpacks the gracious *gift* of suffering. I am challenged to embrace the tender hand of God in times I'd rather pray against the very thing He's using to draw me near. This is a must-read for the body of Christ, one I will turn to again and again.

KIM CASH TATE
Author of *Cling: Choosing a Lifestyle of Intimacy with God*

As the crushed flower yields perfume, so Colleen writes this book. Permeated with scriptural insights discovered and lived in the valley of personal experience, every chapter she writes is designed to help us join her in maximizing the good that God is up to in our suffering. This book will touch you deeply. It will make you laugh and cry. It will refresh you and leave you feeling less alone. It will make you think deeply and give you practical steps you can take in your trials. Above all, it will leave you more in love with your mysteriously wise and loving Savior who is doing something beautiful in you.

MILTON VINCENT
Pastor; author of *The Gospel Primer: Learning to See the Glories of God's Love*

There is an invisible chord that stitches us together, regardless of status or stage of life, net worth, or natural giftings—the string is suffering. Each of us will suffer. The question is, will we suffer well? Will we grit our teeth and bear our sorrow with misery, or will we smile through it with true joy? Colleen knows what it means to endure. She's done it with otherworldly focus, passion, and joy. Let her be your guide through life's dark valley in her beautiful book, *In the Hands of a Fiercely Tender God*. With her trademark combination of wit and wisdom, she will teach you how to hold on more tightly to the One who suffered for you, Jesus Christ.

ERIN DAVIS
Writer, Bible teacher, and fellow sufferer

The Lord chose to refine Colleen Chao in the furnace of affliction. This book is just a tiny glimpse of the resulting beauty that's risen from the ashes. In each page, readers are invited to behold the kindness of the Lord that exists not just in Colleen's battle with terminal cancer, but in every trial and experience of suffering. In the center of the refiner's fire, Christ's followers will assuredly find an abundance of His tender mercies, and this book demonstrates

In the Hands of a Fiercely Tender God

31 Days of Hope, Honesty, and Encouragement for the Sufferer

MOODY PUBLISHERS

CHICAGO

Some content in this book has been adapted from material previously published by the author at colleenchao.com.

All Scripture quotations, unless otherwise indicated, are taken from the Christian Standard Bible, copyright © 2017 by Holman Bible Publishers. Used by permission. Christian Standard Bible® and CSB® are federally registered trademarks of Holman Bible Publishers.

Scripture quotations marked NKJV are taken from the New King James Version®. Copyright © 1982 by Thomas Nelson. Used by permission. All rights reserved.

All emphasis in Scripture has been added.

Edited by Cheryl Molin
Interior design: Brandi Davis
Cover design and illustration: Kelsey Fehlberg

ISBN: 978-0-8024-2990-2

Originally delivered by fleets of horse-drawn wagons, the affordable paperbacks from D. L. Moody's publishing house resourced the church and served everyday people. Now, after more than 125 years of publishing and ministry, Moody Publishers' mission remains the same—even if our delivery systems have changed a bit. For more information on other books (and resources) created from a biblical perspective, go to www.moodypublishers.com or write to:

Moody Publishers
820 N. LaSalle Boulevard
Chicago, IL 60610

5 7 9 10 8 6

Printed in the United States of America

For Eddie and Jeremy—

Only He loves you more than I do.

CONTENTS

FOREWORD

*Y*ou hold a book forged out of sacrificial love. For any sufferer, managing the spiritual, physical, and emotional aspects of suffering is often a full-time job. Suffering is a selfish intruder. It does not care that we have spouses whom we desire to love "till death us do part." Suffering does not leave room for helping our children with homework and soccer games, for kissing boo-boos and packing lunches. Suffering is suffocating. Whether temporal, chronic, or terminal, suffering attempts to suck the life right out of us. That's the tangible side of suffering that is oh so real.

But suffering is also spiritual. Through suffering we identify with our Savior. Through suffering we embark on the road to glory. God's Word assures us that suffering is real, it is regular, it is a resting place for God's Spirit, it reveals God's glory to us, it emboldens us to repentance, it beckons us to live righteously before the Lord and before all, and it is a reminder for us to entrust ourselves fully to our faithful Creator (1 Peter 4:12–19), who is good and does good (Ps. 119:68).

Suffering teaches us that this life is precious and short, but that the glory awaiting us is worth every pain and pill and prognosis. Colleen knows this all too well, and that is why she has written this book for you. With all that her suffering has taken from her, what it has given her is a desire to carve out space and time that she really does not have to help you on your suffering journey.

Like many of you, I'm tempted to compare my light and momentary afflictions to someone else's. I'm tempted to believe that my suffering doesn't equate with the magnitude of a terminal cancer diagnosis or the tragic loss of a loved one. My suffering has not required a hospitalization. I'm tempted to believe that I don't deserve to attend to the reality of my suffering because others are dealing with so much more. In those moments, I'm reminded that while our personal experiences of suffering look different, all Christian sufferers have much in common. In fact, our suffering allows us to see the fullness of the Godhead at work in and through our pain.

God desires to use our suffering to bring glory to Himself, to bring us closer to the suffering of *Christ*, and to help us see the *Spirit's* power at work in the midst of our weaknesses.

As I read chapter after chapter of *In the Hands of a Fiercely Tender God*, my heart felt free to "feel all the feelings," to see how much I really do have in common with fellow sufferers, to embrace my suffering and not shrink back in shame for feeling guilt, fear, or grief over my own season of suffering. I have felt seen and loved and cared for by my dear friend. Her diagnosis may be terminal, but her words of wisdom and encouragement will live on through these pages.

I pray that as you come to know our fiercely tender God through these pages, you will be convinced that living through whatever suffering you must endure is not in vain. I pray that Colleen would know without a shadow of doubt that her living certainly has not been in vain but is a beautiful testimony of suffering that leads her to glory.

KRISTIE ANYABWILE
Bible teacher and author of *Literarily*

INTRODUCTION

*A*t eighteen years old, I had the world on a string.

I could sing and speak to crowds. I'd earned public accolades for my writing. I had endless energy, a strong work ethic, and friends in high places.

And I loved Jesus. I wanted to use all my strengths and giftings to tell the world about Him.

Never in a million years could I have imagined what lay before me: I would spend two decades in the deep waters of anxiety and depression, marry late, suffer twelve years of chronic pain and illness, give birth to a child with health complications, walk through crushing private sorrows, and one day hear those life-altering words:

"You have cancer." And then a few years later—

"Your cancer is back. Stage four. Terminal."

Suffering on its own would have wrecked me. Dark days can poison the soul and rot the bones. But in the hands of a fiercely tender God, suffering has slowly *freed* me, opened my eyes to see eternal realities more clearly, and worked in me inexplicable joy. With each new pain and sorrow, I have come to love and believe Jesus more.

Because I don't naturally have the capacity or skills to suffer well (in fact, I'm a sad, whiny, worrisome sufferer on my own), I've learned I need help along this journey, and lots of it. And at every turn God has provided it: I've learned how to experience Jesus through His Word. I've learned how to glean from the examples of past saints who suffered far more than I have (and suffered with joy). I've learned how to pray through the darkest nights of despair. I've learned practical habits that have helped me to laugh—not just cry—through years of unrelenting crises.

Within these pages are gifts that I've been given in suffering and now I gladly pass along to you, my fellow sufferer. These are the saints, Scriptures, hopes, and habits that have paved my suffering way with great joy. I'm not an authority on the subject of suffering (far from it), but with this book I happily add my voice to the refrain of the multitudes who testify to the fact that God is breathtakingly good to His children on the darkest days and in the deepest pits. He never cheats them. He always outgives them. And if He has entrusted you with suffering, dear one, it is because He loves you beyond anything you can imagine.

May this little book help you to experience His perfect love along your suffering way—

Colleen Chao

one

LOOK

*T*he day we received my first cancer diagnosis, my husband and I sat down with our (then) six-year-old son to tell him the news. Jeremy shed some tears and hugged me tight. I locked eyes with him and said, "This is hard, isn't it, bud? It's not good news. But God is with us, and He turns everything for our good. *Everything.* So, we don't need to fear. And God is going to use this in your life in amazing ways."

Jeremy paused, then asked if we could read the story of "the Fiery Furnace." My husband opened the Bible to Daniel 3 and read of King Nebuchadnezzar's intimidating gold statue, threatening edict, and furious rage at Shadrach, Meshach, and Abednego when they refused to bow down. You know how the story goes: after the men had been bound and thrown into the fiery inferno—

> *King Nebuchadnezzar jumped up in alarm. He said to his advisers, "Didn't we throw three men, bound, into the fire?"*
>   *"Yes, of course, Your Majesty," they replied to the king.*
>   *He exclaimed, "Look! I see four men, not tied, walking around in the fire unharmed; and the fourth looks like a son of the gods."*
> *Dan. 3:24–25*

My husband finished the story and closed the Bible, and after a pause Jeremy said, "There are four of us in this family."

In his suffering, a six-year-old looked and saw that God was with us in our own fiery furnace. He was given eyes to see Jesus standing with us in the flames.

But we're not always so quick to see God with us in the fire, are we? Our eyes are more easily fixed on the pain, the loss, the unfairness. We see the impossible circumstances before us, and we despair, worry, fear, or fume. *God, why have You allowed this furnace to be heated seven times hotter than usual?! Why so much pain? Why the sting of death?*

Isaac Ambrose wrote, "Whilst we look on these things, we cannot see the beauty that is in Christ."[1] While our gaze is fixed on the furnace and the flames, we miss the Son of God whose presence with us in the fire is worth far more than any comfort, any dream fulfilled, any security, any promise of health or relief or rescue. Ambrose continues:

> Oh that all men . . . would presently fall upon the practice of this gospel art of looking unto Jesus! . . . Only Christ is the whole of man's happiness; the sun to enlighten him, the physician to heal him, the wall of fire to defend him, the friend to comfort him, the pearl to enrich him, the ark to support him, the rock to sustain him under the heaviest pressures, "As an hiding-place from the wind, and a covert from the tempest, as rivers of waters in a dry place, and as the shadow of a great rock in a weary land." Isa. 32:2 Come then! let us look on this Sun of righteousness: *we cannot receive harm, but good, by such a look. . . . As Christ is more excellent than all the world, so this sight transcends all other sights; it is the epitome of a Christian's happiness.* (italics added)[2]

In your present suffering, what are you most tempted to fixate on? Is it the apparent unfairness of your situation? *(Why am I afflicted while my friends are so blessed?)* Is it the unrelenting physical pain? The grief that your loved ones must suffer with you? The fact there is no end in sight?

One of the things I love about Christ is that He doesn't ask us to pretend we're *not* in the furnace. Instead, *He joins us there.* He knows it's blazing hot and oppressive and terrifying, and He wants to be with us in it.

When you pass through the waters,
I will be with you,
and the rivers will not overwhelm you.
When you walk through the fire,
you will not be scorched,
and the flame will not burn you.
Isa. 43:2

It may be difficult to look past the flood and the flame today to get a clear view of Jesus. He understands. He's tender to our weakness and weariness. He meets us where we are and won't leave us alone in our pain. *Look!* Here is Jesus, walking with us in our fire—and His presence will change everything.

two

REMEMBER

I remember the spring of 2009—that corner booth in the little café where I met with God before the sun came up every morning. I sat with my coffee, Bible, journal, and C. S. Lewis's *The Problem of Pain*. I experienced the nearness and tenderness of God in a way I've never quite been able to put into words. It was a season of suffering back then too, but those were sacred, otherworldly moments that gave meaning to my pain.

And I remember the summer I was thirty-three and still single. I left behind extremely stressful circumstances to spend three weeks visiting best friends from coast to coast.

We sat in the sun, sipped coffee, took walks, talked late, and laughed hard. I experienced the kindness and joy of Jesus in a way that has marked me ever since.

God tells us so often in Scripture to *remember*—remember who He is and what He has done for us. But suffering can make us forgetful. Our minds are overwhelmed with our present pain or the complexities of surviving another day. We become like a child fixated on his scraped and bleeding knee—in the middle of Disneyland. Caught up in his pain, he loses sight of the magic and marvels all around him.

In the book of Lamentations, the prophet Jeremiah describes suffering that would cause most of us to forget the goodness of God—especially because Jeremiah *attributes his suffering to God.* He says things like,

> *He has driven me away and forced me to walk in darkness instead of light.*
> Lam. 3:2

> *He has laid siege against me, encircling me with bitterness and hardship.*
> v. 5

> *He forced me off my way and tore me to pieces.*
> v. 11

Yikes. Is it okay to say things like this? To tell people that *God* has forced us to walk dark and difficult paths? That *He* is the One who has weighed us down?

I love how raw and real Scripture is, don't you? Haven't we all felt the truth of Jeremiah's words on our darkest days? It's safe to be unedited with God. He can take the full weight of our emotions and questions—and then give us eyes to see things from His perspective. I'm so grateful that Jeremiah was gut honest about his afflictions, but I'm even more grateful that he didn't stop there. Look at what he reminds himself of in the middle of his anguish:

> *Yet I call this to mind,*
> *And therefore I have hope:*
> *Because of the LORD's faithful love*
> *we do not perish,*
> *for his mercies never end.*
> *They are new every morning;*
> *great is your faithfulness!*
> *I say, "The LORD is my portion,*
> *therefore I will put my hope in him."*
>
> *The LORD is good to those who wait for him,*
> *to the person who seeks him. . . .*

For the Lord
will not reject us forever.
Even if he causes suffering,
he will show compassion
according to the abundance of his faithful love.
For he does not enjoy bringing affliction
or suffering on mankind.
Lam. 3:21–25, 31–33

Jeremiah did something astonishingly simple yet powerfully effectual in the midst of his suffering: *he remembered.* He reminded himself of *who God is.* In essence, he was saying, "Self, God isn't happy about my suffering. Nope, that's not His way, that's not His heart. Remember—He is the God of love, mercy, faithfulness, goodness, and compassion! This is not for nothing. Hope again!"

Thousands of years after Lamentations was written, another Jeremiah—Jeremiah Burroughs—wrote in a similar vein:

Name any affliction that is upon you: there's a sea of mercy to swallow it up. If you pour a pail full of water on the floor of your house, it makes a great show, but if you throw it into the sea, there is no appearance of it; so afflictions, considered in themselves, we think they are very great, but let them be considered with the sea of God's mercies we do enjoy, then they are not so much, they are nothing in comparison.[1]

We don't need to pretend our afflictions aren't real and miserable. We just need to put them in the right place— within the "sea of God's mercies." We look (and keep looking) at who He reveals Himself to be in Scripture, and the wonderful things He has done for His people, for *us*.

When have you experienced God's love, kindness, or compassion? Replay that memory in detail today. He came to you in such a beautiful way then; He will come to you again. Sit in that sweet remembrance and let it pour your pailful of pain into His ocean of mercies—mercies that are vast and new every morning.

three

CRY

*B*efore my son spoke his first word, he had physically suffered more than most adults have in their lifetime. Every month he was afflicted with high fevers that left him limp in my arms for long days and nights. His mouth broke out in sores, his joints hurt, and he suffered from chronic skin rashes and intestinal pain. He was intolerant of multiple foods, and what was a "simple cold" for most children meant weeks and months of health complications for Jeremy. I will never forget the night he stopped breathing, and my husband and I rushed him to the emergency room just a mile up the road from us. My precious child, my only son, suffered in ways that wrecked this mama's heart.

On my son's healthier days, I challenged him to develop new skills, stretched him beyond his comfort zone, and delighted to see him do things independently. But on his days of pain and illness, I scooped him into my arms and looked and listened attentively to his every cry and discomfort. Even as a weary, sleepless, often overwhelmed and anxious mama, I wanted to meet his every need, comfort him, track down the best medical care possible. Before he even learned to tell me what was wrong or ask me for what he needed, Jeremy would cry out in his pain for me, and that alone stirred my heart to love in ways I'd never known before.

I can only imagine how much more our Perfect Parent—who is never tired or anxious, who always knows exactly what is wrong with us and what to do about it—longs to care for us when we cry to Him. Imagine how His heart feels when we weep and wail in pain. For years I have loved Isaiah 63:9 for the glimpse it gives us into God's heart: "In all their suffering, he suffered, and the angel of his presence saved them. He redeemed them because of his love and compassion; he lifted them up and carried them all the days of the past."

In all our suffering, He suffers too. C. H. Spurgeon—who lived with chronic illness and pain (as did his wife), who endured slander from envious London pastors, and who wrestled with dark bouts of depression—knew the truth of this. He wrote,

It makes pain so glorious when you think that the very same pain shoots through Him as through you, that there is not so much pain truly in the finger as there is in the head, that the head is indeed the true seat of all the sensitiveness. It is not so much Christ's people who suffer, as it is Christ, Himself, suffering in them.[1]

The God who suffers in you and with you wants you to cry to Him, wants you to "pour out your heart like water before the Lord's presence" (Lam. 2:19; see also Ps. 62:8). Like a small child in pain, you may not have words for your suffering. Maybe sometimes all you can do is writhe and flail, weep and wail. Other times, you can use the words of the psalmists to express your longings. This past week I've cried out to God with these verses:

God of our salvation, help us,
for the glory of your name.
Rescue us . . .
for your name's sake.
Ps. 79:9

31

"Restore us, God;
make your face shine on us,
so that we may be saved."
Ps. 80:3

"Will you not revive us again
so that your people may rejoice in you?
Show us your faithful love, LORD."
Ps. 85:6–7a

"Be gracious to me, Lord,
for I call to you all day long.
Bring joy to your servant's life,
because I appeal to you, Lord.
For you, Lord, are kind."
Ps. 86:3–5a

"LORD, God of my salvation,
I cry out before you day and night.
May my prayer reach your presence;
listen to my cry.
For I have had enough troubles,
and my life is near Sheol."
Ps. 88:1–3

Whether we have words or just groans, we can cry to God knowing He understands our suffering and will carry us through it with His love and compassion.

The beauty of spending so many years crying out to God is that I can look back to see *He has always answered me*—so I can trust He will answer me again. He will love me through this. He will comfort me. Again and again I have experienced the truth of Isaiah 66:13: "As a mother comforts her son, so I [God] will comfort you."

As my son used to cry out for me in his misery—and I would drop everything to comfort and care for him—so I cry out to the God of all comfort (2 Cor. 1:3). And from the depths of your own suffering, you can cry to Him too and experience His perfect comfort once again. Oh, how He loves you.

four

THANK

I owned only one coat until a year ago—and it had spent almost its entire existence in the back corner of my closet. Southern California winters require little more than a sweater, so we wore coats and scarfs just for fun.

But when our family transplanted to a colder climate, we were suddenly shopping for base layers and mid layers and thick socks and *real* coats (because ten-degree weather laughs at SoCal attire). I'm absolutely in love with this cold and snowy winter, but my wardrobe could not look more different than it did a year ago.

It makes me think of how my life's climate has often changed in an instant. Crises have blown in like an Arctic wind and I've found myself in need of a different wardrobe to weather the elements. In fact, I dress vastly differently than I did thirty years ago. And by far one of the best articles of clothing I own for seasons of suffering is gratitude.

However, gratitude is not always easy to put on. Suffering affords me endless opportunities to gripe, to despair, to harden my heart. Some days are so dark, and the pain so acute, that I wonder, *How could there possibly be something good to be thankful for today?*

I've spent the last five years in oncology offices and hospital beds and waiting rooms, surrounded by cancer patients thirty and forty years my senior. I've watched my already thin body drop weight till my bones peeked through my skin. I've been poked and prodded and pumped and scanned and cut till I almost didn't recognize myself. I've lost my headful of hair—twice. At times, it's been physically excruciating to dress myself, to turn over in bed, to walk across a room. Medical bills have exceeded our budget. The list could go on. Cancer has stripped me (and my husband and son) of everything that is normal and stable and "good."

But another reality is at work here, far more real than what my five senses can apprehend. One of the surest ways to experience that unseen reality is to thank God, to nurture a heart of gratitude toward Him. This isn't "positive thinking." This isn't being optimistic or a glass-half-full kind of girl. This is an act of faith.

When we're overwhelmed by affliction, the simplest gratitude may be all we can muster—and it is enough. A small but beautiful moment of belief gently turns our hearts and heads toward our Savior. I can't tell you how many times I've come to a desperately dark moment, completely at the end of myself, and I've sensed the Spirit's gentle nudge, "Thank Me." In response, I've forced myself to thank Him for something seemingly insignificant—"Thank You for this cup of coffee." Then I've added something like, "Thank You for the sunshine streaming through my window." And then with a little more resolve, "Thank You for being with me." Maybe that's all the capacity I have for gratitude in that moment, but more often than not, that simple act of thanksgiving inspires me to thank Him for even more of His gifts and His goodness.

Although my circumstances haven't changed, my perspective has. God knew what He was doing when He commanded us again and again in Scripture to *thank Him*. Thanksgiving is the way we enter into and experience His presence (see Ps. 100:4). To say, "Thank You, God" is to perceive Him with us in our suffering. In reflecting back on the time she and her sister Betsie spent in a Nazi concentration camp, Corrie ten Boom wrote, "Thankfulness keeps us connected to the reality of God in our lives"[1]—even in the darkest corners of a place like Ravensbruck.

This supernatural thanksgiving that connects us to God is a unique kind of gratitude—one that Thomas Watson described as "a work peculiar to a saint. Every bird can sing in spring, but some birds will sing in the dead of winter. Everyone, almost, can be thankful in prosperity, but a true saint can be thankful in adversity."[2]

I long to put on gratitude and sing like a bird in the dead of winter, don't you? Your winter may be strikingly different than mine. Perhaps you've discovered your spouse is having an affair, your child has a drug addiction, or your commitment to honor God as a single person in a couples' world is harder than anyone can imagine. But like me, you've tasted enough of the goodness of God to want more—even though it requires much suffering. To help us sing through our winters, I invite you to join me in cultivating gratitude by recording a daily thanksgiving on page 177 at the back of this book. By doing this, we'll not only train ourselves to look for something to be thankful for each day, but we'll also create a list of gratitude to revisit again and again—a permanent reminder of God's faithfulness to us in our suffering. No matter how small or meager, our thanksgiving will enlarge our hearts to trust Him more, to perceive the reality of God's fiercely tender presence once again.

five

DO

One of the most surprising things about suffering is that the normal stresses of life don't take a vacation just because you're in the thick of it. Amid cancer, we've had to move out of our house due to black mold, my husband's small business has struggled to stay afloat in the wake of COVID, our medical debts have piled up, and my son's health issues have flared.

Sometimes it feels like a Sisyphean task just to make it to the end of a day—let alone think of waking to another just like it.

And our hearts can begin to question the goodness of God when the theme of our life seems to be, "What?! This too? We already passed Way Too Much miles ago!"

As I write this, I wonder what your "too much" is. Maybe you live with a disability that comes with crippling medical expenses, loneliness, and physical pain. Or perhaps you're experiencing a financial reversal that's upending everything in your life—your job, your relationships, your future, your reputation.

How do we summon the courage and endurance to press on through day after day of complex and layered suffering?

I grew up hearing the story of Elisabeth Elliot. She and her husband, Jim, moved to Ecuador to become missionaries, and it was there that Jim was murdered by the Waodani ("Auca") people. As a new widow with a toddler, Elisabeth moved in with the tribe that had killed her husband to show them the love of Christ.

Even as a teen, I was compelled by Elisabeth's story, and I recognized the wisdom she had from years of walking with Christ through uncertainty, grief, and danger. I wanted to know how she did it. I found my answer in one specific piece of her advice—advice she herself had gleaned from an Old Saxon poem:

> *Do it immediately, do it with prayer;*
> *Do it reliantly, casting all care;*
> *Do it with reverence, tracing His Hand*
> *who placed it before thee with earnest command.*

Stayed on omnipotence, safe 'neath His wing,
Leave all resultings, do the next thing.[1]

As a grieving widow with a toddler in the remote jungles of Ecuador, Elisabeth could do nothing about her sorrow and her circumstances, "but doing the next thing, no matter how small, somehow created an impetus that carried her through each long day, one hard hour at a time."[2]

It's been a powerful impetus for me too over these many years—I've been able to "do the next thing" in the muck of circumstances I cannot change. The day after I received my first cancer diagnosis, I did a lot of *hard* things (like calling oncologists and scheduling a slew of appointments) as well as a lot of *mundane* things (like making dinner and washing dishes). And in the unseen places, God was there with me, working His good will in all the awful aspects that were far beyond my control. I couldn't wish away the aggressive lump in my breast. I couldn't protect my husband and son from a grave new suffering. And I couldn't fathom how we were going to walk through cancer after we'd just endured a decade of chronic illness. But I *could* do the next thing—and while I did, I could pray that God would show up bigger than ever.

You may not be able to change your suffering circumstances, but you *can* do whatever lies right in front of you, whether it's mind-numbingly mundane or breathtakingly scary. And in the future, when you look back on these days strung together with a thousand little acts of faith, you will be able to trace the hand of God at work in your darkest hours. He is fiercely and tenderly *for you,* so you can trust Him again today as you "do the next thing."

six

MARVEL

I was a bundle of anxiety. Long years of caring for my sick little boy—with no answers, no cures, and little sleep— had left me fixated on the unsolvable problems in my life. When I sought counsel from a wiser older woman, she gave me unexpected advice. She told me to take an orange and study it carefully: feel the texture of the rind, admire its color, cut it open and smell its fragrance, taste and savor its flavor.

It was the counsel I so badly needed. I'd grown blind to the beauty all around me: sunsets and wildflowers and white-crowned sparrows.

The smell of jasmine in the spring.

The taste of my hot, black decaf coffee in the morning.

Around this same time, I was introduced to the writings of Lilias Trotter. In the late 1800s, Lilias was an incomparably talented artist who caught the attention of John Ruskin. Ruskin said, "She would be the greatest living painter and do things that would be Immortal." Instead, Lilias gave up her auspicious career as an artist and moved to North Africa to serve the God she loved so much.

But even in the harsh climate of her new home, Lilias never lost her love of nature, never stopped looking for and studying the beauty of her surroundings. She sketched paintings of desert life on little corners of paper with her meager supply of colors and brushes. In addition to painting, she wrote eloquently of God's handiwork:

> The baby new moon was hanging in the sunset tonight like a boat for the little angels.
>
> The milky-looking glacier torrent spoke with God's voice this morning.
>
> The morning star is so perfectly marvelous these days. It hangs in the dawn like a great globe of silver fire.
>
> The daisies have been talking again . . .[1]

Lilias's ability to marvel at God in His creation through words and pictures teaches us today "to see with heart-sight as well as eyesight."[2]

Through a wise woman's counsel and the example of Lilias Trotter, I began to rediscover God's breathtaking designs and purposes in the world around me. I took more and more time to stop and look—*really look*—at creation, from the smallest of things to the largest: a leaf, a bug, a mountain, a constellation. As I looked, I marveled. And as I marveled, those monstrous anxieties lost a little momentum.

To marvel is to make God and His beauty bigger than our ugly pain. To marvel is to remember God's care for us by observing how He cares for His lesser creations. It's the remedy for anxiety that Jesus Himself taught His disciples: He told them to "consider the ravens" and "consider how the wildflowers grow" (Luke 12:24, 27).

The Greek word Jesus uses here for "consider" is *katanoeo*—and it means "to consider attentively, fix one's eyes or mind upon; to perceive, remark, observe, understand."[3] Jesus wanted His disciples to perceive through the glory of His creation that "when God does anything, he does it well."[4] He wanted them to know that if God "clothes the grass, which is in the field today and is thrown into the furnace tomorrow, how much more will he do for you—you of little faith?" (Luke 12:28).

Without any effort at all, I can fix my eyes on the hard things, the horrible things of this life. I'm naturally very good at that. But by the power of God's Spirit in me, I can instead fix my eyes and my mind on the handiwork of God. These days, as I ride in the car with my husband and son, or as we take a walk around our neighborhood, I'm constantly pointing out the clouds in the sky, the spindly tree branches, the way the sun hits the water. And if I can't see creation's beauty in person, if I'm stuck in my recliner or in bed, I can still recall how the ocean waves lapped cold and salty against my bare feet—or how that red-tailed hawk rode the air currents, then dove headlong for his tiny prey one hundred feet below him.

What stressor or pain are you fixated on today? If you can, take a few minutes to look out the window or step outside (or watch a scene from a nature documentary!) and marvel at a fiercely tender God who cares for you infinitely more than for the grass, the birds, and the wildflowers.

seven

BELIEVE

*I*magine you could have your dream life. Your loneliness would give way to beautiful belonging, your marriage would be restored, your runaway teen would come home, every one of your relationships would be life-giving and peaceful, you'd be miraculously healed to live a long and healthy life . . .

Now imagine that dream life—but it's devoid of purpose, compassion, and the experience of God's fiercely tender love. Would you still want that life? Would *I* want the chance to live forty more years if those years were emptied of the infinite blessings I'm accumulating in my present suffering? Would I be willing to give up the privilege of caring for other sufferers and showing my son God's goodness in suffering and knowing breathtaking new depths of Jesus' love?

I recently heard the story "Hans in Luck"—a Brothers Grimm fairy tale about a boy who loses all his worldly comforts yet considers himself the luckiest lad in the land. If you're not familiar with the story, here's a brief retelling:

After working faithfully for seven years, Hans asked his employer for his wages so he could return home to his mother. The employer happily gave him "a bag of gold the size of his head,"[1] and Hans set out for home. But the bag of gold was heavy and cumbrous, and it made the journey wearisome—so when Hans happened upon a man riding a horse, and the man offered the horse in exchange for the giant bag of gold, Hans joyfully agreed. Feeling incomparably lucky to not have to walk all the way home, Hans mounted the horse and continued his journey.

But the horse was temperamental, and he reared and bucked and threw Hans to the ground. Discouraged, Hans looked up to see a man walking by with a cow. Gratefully, Hans exchanged his bucking horse for the serendipitous cow, feeling incomparably lucky that he would now have a fresh supply of milk for the rest of his journey.

But the cow produced no milk, and Hans soon exchanged her for a pig (considering himself incomparably lucky to now have an ample supply of sausage and bacon). Then Hans crossed paths with a boy holding a goose. To Hans's dismay, the boy told him that the pig was stolen property. Hans was relieved when the boy offered to return the pig to its rightful owner and give Hans the goose in return. Hans, feeling incomparably lucky at having a goose to take home to his mother—a goose that would provide both food for their tummies and feathers for their bedding—set out again on his way.

Hans met a knife-grinder who told him how he could become wealthy simply by grinding knives. The man talked Hans out of his goose in exchange for the grindstones that would bring him great riches. Once again, Hans set out on his way. But the stones were heavy, and he was tired and thirsty, so when he came across a stream, he eagerly sat down to rest and take a long drink. However, when he set the stones down, they were too near the water's edge and went tumbling into the water.

As he watched the stones sink deeper and deeper into the stream, he

jumped up for joy, and then, kneeling down and returning thanks with tears in his eyes that so mercifully and without any act on his part, and in so nice a way, he had been delivered from the heavy stones, which alone hindered him from getting on. Then, with a light heart and free from every burden, he leaped gaily along till he reached his mother's house.[2]

It's a tongue-in-cheek tale to be sure, and the analogy eventually breaks down—but I wonder if you, like me, can relate to the shortsighted Hans. We begin life carrying a bag heavy with our hopes and dreams, but along the way we end up with what seems like a bum cow or a bag of stones.

*Un*like Hans, though, we don't feel lucky in our losses. Even though we may admit our bag of gold *was* burdensome and unbearable, we're tempted to feel like we've been (dare I say it?)—*cheated* in life. And in our deep disappointment, we wonder at promises in Scripture like these:

> *Those who seek the LORD*
> *will not lack any good thing.*
> *Ps. 34:10*

> *The LORD is my shepherd;*
> *I have what I need.*
> *Ps. 23:1*

> *The LORD grants favor and honor;*
> *he does not withhold the good*
> *from those who live with integrity.*

Happy is the person who trusts in you,
LORD of Armies!
Ps. 84:11–12

God doesn't withhold any good from us, His beloved children. "Yes," we say, "but I've got this horse that won't carry me, this cow that won't give milk, and a bag of stones at the bottom of the sea!" (A special-needs child I don't know how to care for, another failed dating relationship, chronic back pain that keeps me awake at night . . .)

To suffer is to wrestle. To ask the hard questions. To wonder how pain and blessing can coexist. This wrestling has the potential to draw us further into Christ as we take our questions to Him and pour out our hearts to Him (see chapter 3).

But when I *persist in doubting* God's promises of goodness, when I harbor disbelief, I'm succumbing to the lie the serpent whispered to Eve in the very beginning: *Has God really given you everything you need? Isn't God withholding His best from you?*

Faith, on the other hand, is "the reality of what is hoped for, the proof of what is not seen" (Heb. 11:1). Habakkuk—a prophet of God whose suffering made his body tremble, his lips quiver, and his bones feel rotten (Hab. 3:16)—showed us how faith can push through abysmal circumstances to find joy in God:

Though the fig tree does not bud
and there is no fruit on the vines,
though the olive crop fails
and the fields produce no food,
though the flocks disappear from the pen
and there are no herds in the stalls,
yet I will celebrate in the LORD;
I will rejoice in the God of my salvation!
Hab. 3:17–18

Faith is the assurance that there is a reality beyond "right now." Faith says, "I don't understand it all, my heart-eyes don't have 20/20 vision yet, but I *believe* that even as I lose the things dearest to me, God is my greatest treasure and everlasting good. If I have Him, I have everything."

One day soon we will step out of time into eternity and fully understand how much good God has been lavishing on us all along. We'll probably shake our heads and smile ruefully at the bag of gold we clung to at the beginning of our journey, then "jump for joy and give thanks that we were so mercifully delivered from such heavy stones that hindered" our greatest happiness.[3]

Dear fellow sufferer, I invite you to join me today in holding out open hands, relinquishing everything we so desperately want to cling to, and saying by faith, "God, You are good, and what You do is good" (see Ps. 119:68).

God, my heart is so attached to [fill in the blank with your dearest dream, relationship, want, comfort, or ambition], *but I choose to believe that You are good, that You never cheat me, that You always outgive everything I give to You. Help me want* You *above all else. Help me experience Your love in such a way that my heart is fully satisfied in You alone. You are my shepherd; I have everything I need today. I do believe this, Lord—help me in my unbelief! (Mark 9:24). Amen.*

eight

GRIEVE

Last night I stood at my hotel window waving goodbye to my husband and son as they walked across the parking lot below me, then drove away. Tears formed in my eyes as grief struck me with gale force: even the smallest goodbyes these days feel weighty and painful to our family, a foreshadowing of the larger goodbye to come.

Grief is no respecter of person, time, or place. It comes in a thousand shapes and sizes. It finds me midday with my hands buried in a sink full of dishes. It visits me in my dreams. It interrupts a conversation with a friend.

But two little words in the Bible have made all the difference to me in my grief: "Jesus wept" (John 11:35).

This shortest of verses has given me a stunning glimpse into the heart of Christ. It explodes with His love for sufferers. Let's look together at the context for why Jesus wept:

> *Now a man was sick, Lazarus from Bethany. . . . So [his] sisters sent a message to [Jesus]: "Lord, the one you love is sick."*
>
> *When Jesus heard it, he said, "This sickness will not end in death but is for the glory of God, so that the Son of God may be glorified through it."*
>
> *Now Jesus loved Martha, her sister, and Lazarus. So when he heard that he was sick, he stayed two more days in the place where he was.*
> John 11:1, 3–6

Jesus heard that His dear friend was sick to the point of death, *so He stayed away longer.* (Whoa, *what?*) Two days later Jesus told His disciples that Lazarus was dead—and *now* it's time to go to him. (Again . . . what?!) By the time Jesus arrived in Bethany, Lazarus had already been buried for four days, and a crowd had gathered to mourn with Mary and Martha. When the sisters heard that Jesus had arrived, they took turns coming to Him and telling Him, "Lord, if you had been here, my brother would not have died!"

If You had been here. O Lord, if You had been here . . .

Mary was crying, and the Jews with her were crying, and Jesus was "deeply moved in his spirit and troubled" (v. 33). The Greek word here for "deeply moved" (*embrimaomai*) is better translated "to snort with anger."[1] He was troubled by the grief of those around Him, and He was white-hot angry at death. And out of the overflow of His deep emotions, He wept.

Wait. Jesus *knew* He was going to raise Lazarus from the dead, and He *knew* it would bring Him glory, and He *knew* His friends' grief would soon be replaced by the greatest joy. That's why He stayed away in the first place! But, as much as He knew these things, He also hates the curse of death, and He feels others' pain deeply—and so He wept.

Oh, what a comfort this is to me in my own grief. Jesus is not distant or indifferent. Even though He sees the beautiful end to my story of suffering, He isn't just waiting for me at the end of it. He is here now, holding me by the hand and mixing His tears with mine as we walk together.

When C. H. Spurgeon preached on the verse "Jesus wept," he said,

> Jesus is our fellow-sufferer; and this should be our greatest solace. Oh, if we had a High-priest that knew not what it is to suffer as we do, it would be a most unhappy thing for us! If we fled to him for refuge, and found

that he had known no grief, and consequently could not understand us, it would be killing to a broken heart. . . . A Jesus who never wept could never wipe away my tears. That were a grief I could not bear, if he could not have fellowship with me, and could not understand my woe.[2]

The one who grieves knows Jesus in an enviable way. To experience Jesus' comfort and compassion, to feel the depth of His emotions for us, is a sacred thing. Apart from Christ, grief hardens us. But in Christ, grief enlarges our hearts to know and love Him more.

Last night I stepped back from my hotel window with tears in my eyes and pain in my heart. *O God, I can't bear the thought of saying goodbye to my boys for good. I don't want to leave them this soon.* But I sensed Jesus with me, tender to my grief and all that this journey is requiring of me, of us. And because He too has known grief, because He too has wept, because He too has hated the last enemy, Death, He was able to comfort and quiet me.

He is able to comfort and quiet you too, my fellow sufferer. Not only is He able, but He also *longs* to. Today may you feel safe to grieve with Him and shelter yourself in the tenderness of His embrace. He loves you so.

nine

TRUST

I graduated from high school eager to begin college at my dream school in San Diego. However, I realized that, despite generous scholarships, I would still need to take a school loan to swing the full tuition, room, and board. With my heart set on moving overseas after college, to serve people in impoverished places (and consequently to live on a shoestring budget), I painstakingly decided against the loan and opted instead to stay home and work full time for a year. I would sock away my earnings to attend college loan-free the following year.

Back then, there was no such thing as a "gap year" between high school and college, so what I did was unpopular and criticized. I was hired at a local theological seminary, where I worked as a receptionist and rubbed shoulders with remarkable professors, staff, and students. Despite scoring a fantastic job, it was a difficult year, and I was often depressed. I felt trapped, almost imprisoned, by my unconventional decision and circumstances. The year that had once promised me my independence and freedom instead was making my world suffocatingly small and confined.

But I found solace in a little trail through the beautiful seminary campus. On my lunch hours I walked around a pond full of lazy ducks and under shady pines, past brilliant bougainvillea and beside bubbling hot springs. As I walked, I talked to God. And His presence pierced through my depression and disappointment and slowly began transforming a difficult year into a hallowed one.

I was on the cusp of learning, in a much smaller way, what Joseph of Genesis had learned when he was in his late teens. Joseph, son of Jacob, and great-grandson of Abraham. The seventeen-year-old dreamer who had visions of greatness. The young man whose world came crashing down into a pit, whose dreams dissipated into slavery and then imprisonment, whose reputation was wrecked and freedom unjustly stolen. Joseph—the sufferer who experienced God with him in his pit, with him in his temptation, with him in his prison. Four times

Genesis 39 tells us, *"The LORD was with Joseph."* Betrayal and slavery and imprisonment should have turned the teenage dreamer into a hard-hearted, bitter man. Instead, Joseph emerged from his thirteen years of suffering a wise, forgiving, faith-filled visionary. Why? Because "the Lord was with Joseph."

I love how Samuel Rutherford describes this kind of experience. A Scottish professor and pastor in the 1600s, he, like Joseph, suffered a period of exile, as well as indescribable grief (he lost his first wife and *seven of his nine children*)—yet he wrote, "Christ and His cross together are sweet company. My prison is my palace, my losses are rich losses, my pain easy pain, my heavy days are holy and happy days. I may tell a new tale of Christ to my friends."[1]

"My prison is my palace." How could he say such a thing? How do you mourn the loss of your spouse and seven of your children and conclude, "My heavy days are happy days"? Because, like Joseph, he had experienced the presence of Christ with him in his sufferings, and that had transformed his worst circumstances into a "palace" of holiness and happiness.

Joseph of Egypt and Samuel of Scotland, separated by thousands of years, both endured loss and tragedy and imprisonment, and came out on the other side with a tender heart and a tenacious faith—not because they excelled at suffering, but because of the fiercely tender presence of God with them in the pit, with them in prison, with them in the graveyard. I look back at my eighteen-year-old self and see how God's presence turned my first bout with deep disappointment and depression, my first encounter with "the real world," into a place of transformation. Greater sufferings lay ahead, but God was gently teaching me how to trust Him, how to perceive His presence in my depression, how to experience Him in my disappointment.

What is your "prison" today? Where do you feel trapped or disappointed or deeply grieved? Spend a few minutes talking to God about your circumstances, asking Him to help you trust Him and to sense His presence with you in your pain.

God is our refuge and strength,
a helper who is always found
in times of trouble.
Therefore we will not be afraid,
though the earth trembles
and the mountains topple
into the depths of the seas,
though its water roars and foams
and the mountains quake with its turmoil. Selah. . . .

The LORD of Armies is with us;
the God of Jacob is our stronghold. Selah.
Ps. 46:1–3, 7

ten

SORROW

I'll never forget the first time sorrow found me. I was ten years old when the phone rang with terrible news: my cousin, Ian, had been killed in a freak accident. As a pastor's kid, I'd been around death and attended funerals routinely, but *this* death and *this* funeral were different. They hurt. They made me realize life was unfair and fragile.

As I passed from childhood into adulthood, I came to understand that sorrow would always be woven into the fabric of life—it comes in a thousand shades, and it colors all our days. As the psalmist wrote, "Our lives last seventy years or, if we are strong, eighty years. Even the best of them are struggle and sorrow; indeed, they pass quickly and we fly away"

(Ps. 90:10). Sometimes sadness stacks upon sadness, grief upon grief, till it's hard to believe there could be anything good left in the world. But a precious hope holds us fast, even on the darkest days: we can sorrow, we can grieve and mourn, knowing *it's a passing reality*—it's a temporary grief.

Amy Carmichael was a Scottish single woman who moved to India in the 1800s to spend her life rescuing children who had been sold into temple prostitution—and providing them with a home and a mother's love. She spent the final twenty years of her life bedridden and in constant pain. Out of her own suffering, and the suffering she had witnessed all around her, she wrote:

> Joy, not suffering, is eternal. . . . Joy is given; sorrow is lent. . . . It is lent to us for just a little while that we may use it for eternal purposes. Then it will be taken away and everlasting joy will be our Father's gift to us, and the Lord God will wipe away all tears from off all faces (Isa. 25:8).
>
> So let us use this "lent" thing to draw us nearer to the heart of Him who was once a Man of Sorrows (He is not that now, but He does not forget the feeling of sorrow). Let us use it to make us more tender with others, as He was when on earth and is still, for He is touched with the feeling of our infirmities (Heb. 4:15).[1]

As much as sorrow is painful, it is even more *profitable.* We sufferers who love Jesus live in an eternal economy where brief sorrows are exchanged for infinite joys. Sorrow never feels brief at the time (on the contrary, time passes oh-so-slowly for the sorrower), but in light of forever, it is a mere millisecond. Like I've often explained to my son—the pain that feels excruciating here will feel like the tiniest pinch in eternity (if that), and it will have earned for us reward beyond our imagination. That's the promise of 2 Corinthians 4:17: "For our momentary light affliction is producing for us an absolutely incomparable eternal weight of glory."

These afflictions that cause us to sorrow deeply, to lay awake through the night in our grief, to feel burdened beyond our capacity—one day they will give way to so much goodness and joy that it will take an eternity for us to experience it all (which means we will never reach the end of it).

C. H. Spurgeon put it this way: "The more sorrow the more joy. If we have loads of sorrow, then the Lord's power will turn them into tons of joy."[2]

We are merely borrowing today's sorrow, but soon we'll exchange it for gifts loaded with glory—gifts that can never be taken away from us. This sorrow on loan is being used to work miracles in our heart; it's drawing us further in to the heart of the Man of Sorrows, to the One who "bore our sicknesses" and "carried our pains" (Isa. 53:4). He sees, He understands, He is with us to help us carry our griefs—and one day soon He will turn it all into "tons of joy."

eleven

GO

*I*t's a strange thing writing of "suffering" in our first-world American context where most of us don't daily fear for our lives, wonder where our next meal is coming from, or risk persecution for our faith. I know *so little* of suffering when I think about people like Ann Judson (who left behind all her worldly comforts to serve God in a hostile land, lost her first baby at birth, her second child at seventeen months, and then died when her third child was not yet two years old)[1]— or when I hear about modern-day victims of trafficking, slavery, and warfare. I'm tempted to despair over my "softness." When people tell me they're amazed at how I'm handling stage-four cancer, I'm deeply encouraged—but I also squirm a little under the compliment. I know myself far too well to be impressed with *me*. I'm constantly, keenly aware that *God* is sustaining me—and that my circumstances could be far worse than they are.

But here's the thing that we sufferers all share in common, no matter how big or small our pain: *none of us are good at suffering*. None of us have the capacity to endure hardship with hope and joy. But the secret to slowly becoming a hope-filled, joyful sufferer has been shockingly simple (not easy, but simple): *I go to God*. Again and again . . . and *again*.

I go to Him when I'm struggling with His will for me.

I go to Him in the middle of the night when grief threatens to undo me.

I go to Him when I'm throwing myself an epic pity party.

"Going to Him" means turning my thoughts to Him and telling Him exactly what I'm feeling, in all the nitty gritty, gory details. I open my Bible to engage with God—and with the smallest mustard seed of faith, I believe that He's listening to me and that He will be able to do something about my suffering.

That rhythmic act of going to Him softens my heart, gives me an ear to hear His voice, and helps me exchange my self-absorbed monologues for beautiful *dialogues* with Him.

Here's what I've become increasingly convinced of through

this process over decades now: I cannot hear from Him or dialogue with Him (and thus have no hope of suffering well) *apart from His Word.* Through the pages of Scripture He speaks exactly what my heart needs to hear. He reveals Himself (sometimes in ways I don't immediately recognize), and those revelations change *everything*—my thoughts and desires and perspective and all. And herein lies one of the most sacred gifts of suffering: the sufferer has a unique capacity to know God through His Word in ways that cannot be experienced through days of comfort and ease. C. H. Spurgeon put it this way:

> Prosperity is a painted window which shuts out much of the clear light of God, and only when the blue, and the crimson, and the golden tinge are removed, is the glass restored to its full transparency. Adversity thus takes away tinge, and colour, and dimness, and we see our God far better than before, if our eyes are prepared for the light. . . . In the absence of other goods the good God is the better seen.[2]

In the hands of a fiercely tender God, suffering is a gift. It's the acetone-drenched rag that cleans the painted window blocking our view of Him. And nothing on earth is more precious than seeing and knowing and loving Jesus more through our suffering (Phil. 3:10). Slowly, sometimes awkwardly, suffering allows us to see Him more clearly because we are forced to go to Him again and again.

Over the past several months our family has been hard pressed on every side, not just by cancer but also by a number of other stressors and heartaches. (Jeremiah Burroughs so aptly wrote, "It is very rare that one affliction comes alone; commonly, afflictions are not single things, but they come one upon the neck of another."[3]) Yesterday I was both sad and angry over the unrelenting hardships, and I felt weak and needy. But I went to God repeatedly throughout the day and He spoke to my hurting heart, revealing His nearness and goodness yet again.[4]

So, from one weak person to another, here is my strong encouragement, especially if you feel like your present sufferings are far beyond your capacity: *keep going to God.* Tell Him everything you're feeling, raw and unedited. He can take it. Trust that He never belittles us for our kindergarten capacity to suffer. He never says, "Well, *Susie* could handle this so much better than *you*!" On the contrary, He is compassionate and patient, strong and ready to help us in our time of need.

For their compassionate one will guide them,
and lead them to springs. . . .
For the LORD has comforted his people,
and will have compassion on his afflicted ones.
Isa. 49:10, 13b

twelve

WAIT

*H*ave you heard the old French tale of a boy named Peter? One day an impatient schoolboy escaped to the forest, where he met an old lady who gave him a magic ball, out of which protruded a delicate silver thread. She promised him that every time he pulled the thread, time would jump forward. Peter was beside himself with joy. Finally, those long, wearisome school days would be blissfully short. (Recess and lunch only!) Peter quickly realized the magic ball's usefulness extended far beyond the classroom: When he grew impatient to marry his high school sweetheart—he tugged at the thread. When he wearied of looking for a job—he tugged at the thread. When the babies cried through the night—*tug*.

73

When marriage grew difficult—*tug*. When the kids grew older and made bad decisions that broke his heart—*tug*. When sickness came—*tug*.

And so it went till Peter suddenly found himself an old man on his deathbed, and he was grieved by the gifts of time and relationship he had squandered. While he had spared himself the suffering and mundanity of life, he was little changed from that impatient schoolboy of yesteryear—and in avoiding all hardship, he had missed out on life's greatest gifts.

Today if someone handed me a magic ball with a silver thread, I would be sorely tempted to tug at it. I would happily fast-forward through this difficult day if I could. But thank God, I cannot. This day is a gift in disguise. Right here in the muck of misery there is a front row seat to watch God work miracles on my behalf. Isaiah 64:4 says, "From ancient times no one has heard, no one has listened to, no eye has seen any God except you who acts on behalf of the one who waits for him."

The God of wonders—the God no eye nor ear can fathom—loves working on our behalf. But for us to experience His work in our lives, we can't rush past our pain. (No magic silver balls allowed!) We have to stay in the pain and wait. And wait. And sometimes wait some more. God is not in a mad dash to the finish line as we so often are. He knows exactly what should happen and when it should happen and how it should happen—so that we experience the absolute highest happiness in Him. (As Isaiah 30:18 tells us, "All who wait patiently for him are happy.")

Waiting doesn't mean dawdling. It's not sluggish nor inactive. Rather, it's the willingness to walk with Jesus *through* suffering, not *around* it. It is actively believing that God will not waste one moment of our affliction. And when we wait—when we sit long in the suffering—we can bank on the fact that the incomparable God is working His wonders for us (even if we can't quite see them yet).

Today, if you're tempted by a magic ball with a silver thread, you're not alone. Waiting is hard, even wearisome, work. But it's glorious work too. It's the stuff miracles are made of. May God give us hearts to wait long on Him—and anticipate the wonders He is working for us.

thirteen

CONFESS

*A*s a single woman, I frequently heard married people say that singleness was a result of discontentment—and that once you were content, God would bless you with a spouse. This obviously was not biblical, nor was it true to my own experience. During my years of singleness, there were weeks and months at a time when I experienced amazing, beautiful contentment—when I didn't have to daily fight for it—but still no husband arrived. Moreover, *all* of us, whether married or single, struggle with contentment in a variety of ways in every season of life. So, although I knew God wasn't punishing me for my sin while rewarding my friends for their sin*less*ness, remaining single seven to twelve years longer than my friends gave me ample opportunity to *detect* my discontentment and *deal* with it regularly. See the difference there? I wasn't single because I was discontent, but singleness helped me see and confess my discontentment.

The Bible is clear that suffering is not necessarily a result of someone's sin (see Luke 13:2–3; John 9:3; 2 Cor. 12:7), but I have found that suffering always gives me enviable opportunities to see my sin more clearly and deal with it more ruthlessly.

- God has used chronic illness to help me identify envy and resentment in my heart, confess those sins, and slowly learn to "keep my eyes in my own lane" as one wise woman put it.

- He's used relational conflicts to help me see my selfishness and wrongs, confess them, and learn how to unconditionally love and forgive.

- He's used cancer to help me recognize what a vise grip I have on this world, confess it (again and again), and live into realities beyond what I can see and feel.

Confession of sin is a beautiful gift of suffering. Pain and sorrow and wearisome waits can reveal to us what otherwise might go undetected (and ruin us in the long run). In Psalm

119:67, David wrote, "Before I was afflicted I went astray, but now I keep your word." And Thomas Watson expounded on this when he wrote,

> Affliction teaches what sin is. In the word preached, we hear what a dreadful thing sin is, that it is both defiling and damning, but we fear it no more than a painted lion; therefore God lets loose affliction, and then we feel sin bitter in the fruit of it. A sick bed often teaches more than a sermon. We can best see the ugly visage of sin in the glass of affliction. Affliction teaches us to know ourselves. In prosperity we are for the most part strangers to ourselves. God makes us know affliction, that we may better know ourselves.[1]

God is not wielding a club of pain to punish us. He is wisely, tenderly taking the scalpel of suffering to remove life-threatening tumors and cataracts and diseases of the heart—to give us more health and wholeness than we've ever known before. He is the greatest and kindest of all physicians.

fourteen

FORGIVE

*I*n my twenties, I had two friends who were chronically sick. I was generally healthy at the time, so I secretly chafed at all their talk about symptoms and aches and pains. I doubted their food allergies were real. I thought that if they just stopped thinking about all their maladies, they would disappear. On the outside, I appeared patient and kind, a good friend who listened with compassion. On the inside, I might have rolled my eyes once or twice.

But by the time I turned thirty-two, irritating little physical symptoms I'd ignored for years were exploding into chronic pain, food intolerances, and one illness after another. I cringed at how compassionless I'd once been with my ailing friends. I'd missed such precious opportunities to sincerely enter in with them, to really hear and understand them, to comfort them. With this in mind, I disclosed very little of my own physical sufferings to anyone, fully expecting others to respond as I had—impatiently with a little eye-rolling.

As time went on, I had to cancel more and more commitments, and my world grew increasingly smaller. Soon it was apparent that several friends were angry with me. On one hand, I couldn't blame them, but on the other hand, it hurt. I didn't have words to explain how complex my life had become. How could I make sense of it to those who were so healthy, who were dancing circles around me?

Even though I'd failed others in similar ways myself, even though I understood where these friends were coming from, forgiveness didn't come easily to me. When we're bearing up under weighty burdens, it's difficult to deal with the insensitivities and failings of those close to us—those we long to have in our corner, fighting with us and for us. And the heavier the burden, the fewer the friends who will be able to enter into the suffering with us. Ironically, the greater our suffering, the more opportunities we'll have to forgive.

Even the people closest to you may not know how to show up for you in your grief, and their silence will be deafening. Others may show up *too* much and speak true-but-untimely words (think Job's friends, Job 12:1–5; 16:1–5). Still others may be convinced they know exactly what you need in your suffering but miss the mark by a long shot. Haven't we *all* been guilty of all of these? We've been silent when we should have said something. We've said too much. We've barged in with help that wasn't helpful. Our capacity to forgive is enlarged when we remember that we are equally guilty of failing our fellow sufferers.

In fact, if my failures and sins (first and foremost against God, then against others) filled up all the pages in all the books in the New York Public Library, by comparison, a friend's sins against me would fit on a little index card. God burned down my library of sin, left no trace or memory of it, and never brings it up in our conversation—so how in the world can I make much ado about a measly little 3″ x 5″ piece of paper?

The apostle Paul wrote, "Be kind and compassionate to one another, forgiving one another, just as God also forgave you in Christ" (Eph. 4:32). In his sermon on this passage, C. H. Spurgeon said,

> Now observe how the apostle puts it. Does he say "forgiving another"? No, that is not the text, if you look at it. It is "forgiving, one another." One another! Ah, then that

means that if you have to forgive to-day, it is very likely that you will yourself need to be forgiven to-morrow, for it is "forgiving one another." It is turn and turn about, a mutual operation, a co-operative service. . . . You forgive me, and I forgive you, and we forgive them, and they forgive us, and so a circle of unlimited forbearance and love goes round the world. There is something wrong about me that needs to be forgiven by my brother, but there is also something wrong about my brother which needs to be forgiven by me, and this is what the apostle means—that we are all of us mutually to be exercising the sacred art and mystery of forgiving one another.[1]

I love Christ's example of forgiveness. It's breathtaking. He too had friends who failed Him: they fell asleep while He sweated blood, they abandoned Him in His greatest hour of need, and in general they *just didn't get it.* Not only that, He had enemies who mocked Him, abused Him, and killed Him. And He forgave them *all*, from the most unfaithful friends to the most cold-blooded enemies.

He understands how we feel (and then some), but He also shows us the way of His heart—lavish, liberating forgiveness. Wounds from a friend allow us to experience more of Him in the God-shaped spaces of our soul where no one else belongs. We can let others off the hook because we have been let off the hook—and because God is the truest friend, the greatest comforter, and the sweetest presence. *He never fails,* and He wants us to experience that reality to the marrow of our soul.

Who has wounded or failed you in your suffering? You can bring their offenses before God today, tell Him how you feel (how you're sad or mad or anxious), and then ask Him to help you practice again "the sacred art and mystery of forgiving."[2]

fifteen

LET GO

*A*s soon as I heard my cancer was back and it was terminal this time, I knew what I needed to do: *prioritize*. With my days on earth being cut short, I resolved to be even more strategic about where I invested my limited time, energies, and resources. I quickly created several "circles": my husband and son in my inner circle; my (big!) family and five best friends in my second circle; and in my third circle, a few close friends, as well as a few dear ones I want to continue reaching out to and caring for. I determined that if I had extra time and energy, I would move on to those friends and acquaintances in successive circles.

My younger self would have been appalled at this kind of ruthless prioritizing. It would have seemed selfish and unspiritual. But over the years I've slowly learned the wisdom of knowing my limitations and letting go of peripheral things so that I can hold fast to the most important things. I love how Richard Sibbes put it:

> Christ makes us wise to ponder and weigh things, and to rank and order them accordingly, so that we may make the fitter choice of what is best. . . . We should judge of things as to whether they help or hinder our main purpose; whether they further or hinder our judgment; whether they make us more or less spiritual, and so bring us nearer to the fountain of goodness, God himself.[1]

Even Jesus, when He was on earth, didn't heal every sick person or preach in every city. He chose only twelve men to be in His inner circle. He had the ability to love the very people who rejected Him, even while letting them go (see Mark 10:21–22). The infinite God of no limitations chose to confine Himself to a human body with many limitations and weaknesses. In this way, He became like us so He could understand what it is to be weak and limited.

This is especially precious truth for the sufferer, because in seasons of hardship, far more is demanded of us than makes sense to others. Not everyone will understand why we're struggling to crawl through days we used to waltz through. It's taken me a long time to learn to accept my limitations, but it's taken me even longer to accept the fact that my limitations may be part of God's good plan for others. Ultimately, no one needs me—but they do need God. And He will be to them what I cannot be. He will gently teach them that their happiness does not depend on me, and He will often raise up someone else who can care for them better than I could have. I rest in the question once posed to me by one of my best friends: "What's wrong with weakness?"

Indeed—what's wrong with it? What's wrong with being weak and limited? All this letting go frees our hands to hold more tightly to the One who "knows what we are made of, remembering that we are dust" (Ps. 103:14). Even if others want us to be made of muscle and moxie, even if we deeply disappoint people because of our frailties, God gently draws us into His embrace and says, "You don't have to be God. Leave that to Me. I'm with you, and I have everything you need for this."

Colossians 1:17 promises us God is holding everything together—which means *we don't have to*. We can let go of unnecessary expectations and unrealistic demands and keep as priority those things God has pressed into our hearts. The relationships God calls us to, He gives us grace for—and what there is grace for will "bring us nearer to the fountain of goodness, God himself."[2]

sixteen

LAUGH

I was born with laughter in my bones. My grandparents on both sides of the family were witty with a dry sense of humor, which they passed along to my parents. And I spent my growing-up years surrounded by church and family friends who would make me laugh till my abs ached. I'm smiling as I remember Bert, Bill, Scott, Darryl, Rocky, Ray, and Karen—and the gift of laughter they gave me in my early years.

But life can wear us down, and the heavier and harder it gets, the more our youthful spirit waxes and wanes. I once heard a wise old woman say, "We weren't baptized in vinegar!" But as our dreams for life turn on their head, and sorrows and disappointments burden our days, life can start to feel like we're bathing in apple cider vinegar. There are even seasons when laughter begins to feel like *a luxury*.

I remember one evening, in my late thirties, after two years of nonstop illness and insomnia, a job loss, our apartment flooding, multiple moves, and the deaths of several loved ones, *I laughed one night*—just a short burst of a laugh, but the sound was strange to my ears. I looked at my husband and my toddler to see if they were as shocked by the sound as I was. I hadn't laughed in a long, long time. I'd forgotten *how* in all the sadness.

Maybe that was good. Maybe it was me becoming more like Jesus because He was a "Man of Sorrows." Maybe laughter was excessive and trivial in light of all the pain.

But the more I studied the life of Christ, the more I became convinced that fishermen and tax collectors and prostitutes aren't drawn to the company of a grim and grave man; the masses won't travel great distances and go without food all day to listen to an uptight teacher. Rather, they're drawn to engaging, joyful, authentic personalities, of which Jesus was the ultimate. Yes, He was a Man of Sorrows, but He was also more joyful than any of His companions (see Ps. 45:7). In fact, throughout Scripture we find a singing, feasting, rejoicing God:

In your presence is abundant joy; at your right hand are eternal pleasures.

P_{S}. 16:11

As a groom rejoices over his bride, so your God will rejoice over you.

Isa. 62:5

On this mountain, the LORD of Armies will prepare for all the peoples a feast of choice meat, a feast with aged wine, prime cuts of choice meat, fine vintage wine.

Isa. 25:6

"Blessed is the one who will eat bread in the kingdom of God!"

Luke 14:15

"He will rejoice over you with gladness. . . . He will delight in you with singing."

Zeph. 3:17

We don't serve a miserable, sorrowful God. The longer I've known Him and experienced His presence in my life, the more authentically I laugh—because there is more joy and pleasure in His presence than in any other person or place or circumstance I've ever known. Suffering with Jesus has seasoned my laughter and grown it large with hope and freedom and peace I didn't have twenty years ago. When I laugh now, it's as if my heart is saying, "Pain, you haven't won! Grief, get back in your place. God is writing a good story, and He wins in the end!"

Dear sufferer, we laugh because He made us in His image—and *He laughed first*. He is a God of laughter. He smiles more than He frowns. He rejoices over us. He delights in us. He spreads a feast for us. And suffering is one way He draws us deeper into Himself and further into His joy. An easy, comfortable life might actually be the biggest hindrance to a life of rich and beautiful laughter—but suffering in Jesus' presence is the secret to why we "can laugh at the time to come" (Prov. 31:25).

seventeen

UNRAVEL

*H*ave you heard the Ukrainian tale of "The Mitten"? While collecting firewood in the dead of winter, a boy unknowingly drops his warm woolen mitten in the middle of a snowy forest. Soon a small mouse discovers it and burrows into it, taking shelter from the biting cold. Not long after, a frog happens upon the mitten, and he squeezes in beside the mouse. Then, in frigid succession, an owl, a rabbit, a fox, a big gray wolf, a wild boar, and a bear discover the mitten and squeeze themselves in as well. Finally, a little old cricket with creaky, aching legs happens upon the mitten and says to herself, "Now that looks like a nice warm place. I'll just hop over and see if I can squeeze in, too!"

But ah me, that was all that was needed to finish off the poor old mitten. The cricket had no more than put her first scratchy foot inside when, with a rip and a snap, the stitches came apart, the old leather cracked, and the soft red lining split in half, popping all the animals into the snow![1]

For the past year since my second, and terminal, cancer diagnosis, there have been weeks on end when God has given me (and my husband and son) a supernatural mitten of seemingly endless capacity to hold rabbits and owls and foxes and wolves and bears, to stretch and flex and expand in ways that truly seem miraculous. But then, every month or two, along comes Little Old Cricket Week and, with a rip and a snap, the stitches come apart and the lining splits in half and everything comes spilling out. On those weeks I'm overwhelmed by the myriad sorrows and stresses and feats of this journey—"animals" that just moments before I was able to accommodate with grace and joy. But the ripping and the splitting are a good and necessary part of this process because they remind me how fragile I am apart from God holding me together. If I perpetually bore up under maximum capacity with joyful strength, I'd begin to think there was something inherently amazing about me. Instead, on Little Old Cricket Week, I see again how extraordinary it is that God is sustaining me through what is utterly impossible to bear myself. On my own, I am tragically weak and limited, constantly living at the edges of my undoing. But it's at those very edges that I experience the power of God in and through me.

Susannah Spurgeon, wife of C. H. Spurgeon, also knew what it was to be weak and frayed, to live at the edges of herself. She was an invalid who rarely made it to church to hear her husband preach. She was married to a great man, a famous man, a man who wrestled with the demon of depression, and who himself suffered from physical illness (gout). Susannah adored her husband—so when he died eleven years before she did, she suffered tremendously. In a devotion she wrote after Charles's death, she explained why "the tearing" was necessary:

> The lesson set before us may be, "He has torn, He has smitten;" "He makes sore, He wounds;" and in our own experience, we may feel how painful is the truth thus taught. But if the eye of faith can discern the precious postscripts which follow, "He will heal," "He will bind us up," "His hands make whole," we are strengthened to endure patiently the trial which is so sure to end in

triumph; and we say, "Ah, Lord! You do but frown—to make Your smile the sweeter! You do kill—only that You may make alive! Blessed wounding, gracious suffering, which places us under the great Physician's love and care!"

'Tis worth the tearing to be tended
By hands so gentle in their touch;
Pains and griefs are sweetly ended;
Can I praise You, Lord, too much?[2]

When Susannah referred to the tearing and the wounding, she was quoting from Hosea 6:

Come, let's return to the LORD.
For he has torn us,
and he will heal us;
he has wounded us,
and he will bind up our wounds.
He will revive us after two days,
and on the third day he will raise us up
so we can live in his presence.
Hos. 6:1–2

Today if you feel like your suffering is causing you to un-ravel, I hope these words are a gentle reminder that God's purpose in this pain is to heal you and bind you up and draw you further into His presence. He's already conquered the grave and raised you up by giving His precious Son for you. *How much more* will He do for you now that you are His favored child?

eighteen

ASK

The summer of 2017 was the first time in a decade that I felt *well.* I was tucking in more than three hours of sleep each night, I had energy, and the aches and pains of chronic illness were minimal. On top of that, my six-year-old's health had improved enough for us to experience the edges of normalcy. My husband and I looked at each other and whispered with relief, "We're not in crisis mode anymore!"

But as I showered before church on a midsummer Sunday morning, I felt a little lump in my right breast. My eyes filled with tears as I wondered, *What if this is cancer? After all we've been through, what if we're about to face our biggest health crisis yet? God wouldn't do that to us, would He?*

We began a long and complicated testing process. Some days I had miraculous calm and confidence in God's goodness. Other days I couldn't loosen fear's vise-grip on my heart.

Don't make me walk this, Lord, I begged Him.

And then just as quickly I would add, *But if this is where You are going, I want to go with You. I don't want to miss out on what You're doing.*

Even in the scariest moments, holding my breath for that decisive phone call, mind racing, body trembling—I knew He was with me. And as I hid myself in Him during those waiting weeks, His Spirit clearly impressed upon my spirit: "This lump is a gift."

What kind of gift, I could not fathom. As we continued to test and wait (and test and wait some more), I hoped for the best, but readied my heart for the worst. Because what if the worst *was* the gift?[1]

Early in those fourteen weeks of testing, I made a trip to an imaging specialist in San Diego. When I saw the images of my scans that day—I knew. There was no doubt. It was cancer. I got into my car, trembling from head to toe, and began my ninety-minute drive home. As I drove, I poured out my heart to God—and while I forget most of what I said to Him that day, I will never forget crying out to Him again and again, "Give me more joy and peace than I've ever experienced before."

It wasn't a timid question: "Would You give me joy and peace, God?" It was a bold request: "If this is where we're going together, I'm going to need You to give me what I can't conjure up on my own." In those moments, God's presence seemed to fill every inch of my car. He was surrounding me. He was holding me together. And even as my body trembled and my heart quaked, I knew He was prompting me to cry out for the impossible as we set out for places I did not want to go. He wanted to give me mind-blowing gifts—but first He wanted me to boldly ask Him for them.

And here's the thing about gifts from God: they're not meant for us alone—*they're meant to be shared.* Like the depression and singleness and chronic illness that preceded it, cancer was to usher me into the sacred places of others' sufferings, allowing me to be a conduit of Christ's compassion and comfort and love. F. B. Meyer said, "The grave may be dark and deep, the winter long, the frost keen and penetrating; but spring will come, and the stone be rolled away, and the golden stalk shall wave in the sunshine, bearing its crown of fruit, and *men shall thrive on the bread of our experience, the product of our tears and suffering and prayers*" (italics added).[2]

For the past five years, cancer has been just that: dark and long, keen and penetrating—but all these tears and pains and prayers have been turned not only for my own good, but also for the good of other sufferers. It is the beauty of 2 Corinthians 1:3–7 at work:

> Blessed be the God and Father of our Lord Jesus Christ, the Father of mercies and the God of all comfort. He comforts us in all our affliction, so that we may be able to comfort those who are in any kind of affliction, through the comfort we ourselves receive from God. For just as the sufferings of Christ overflow to us, so also through Christ our comfort overflows. If we are afflicted, it is for your comfort and salvation. If we are comforted, it is for your comfort, which produces in you patient endurance of the same sufferings that we suffer. And our hope for you is firm, because we know that as you share in the sufferings, so you will also share in the comfort.

Even as I live in the cruelty of this terminal diagnosis, I am forever grateful God gave me the "gift of cancer." No, cancer itself is not a gift—it's a curse that would have ruined me. But God has taken that curse and transformed it into *countless* gifts. *Immeasurably good gifts* that will follow me into eternity. As for the joy and peace I begged God for five years ago, they have come in stunning proportions. He has outgiven everything I asked Him for. Anxiety still pays me the occasional visit, depression peeks his head in every now and then, but joy and peace reign. If you knew me and my history with anxiety and depression, you would understand that is nothing short of *miraculous*.

God loves working miracles on behalf of His suffering children. We see proof of this throughout Scripture and throughout history. Our deepest sorrows, our sharpest pains, are right where God wants to outgive us with His breathtakingly good gifts. It was Lilias Trotter who wrote, "Take the very hardest thing in your life—the place of difficulty, outward or inward, and expect God to triumph gloriously in that very spot. Just there He can bring your soul into blossom!"[3]

Whatever your suffering may be, you can ask God to do miracles in you and for you and for those your life touches—miracles of the heart and soul that will echo into eternity. Even as our hearts quake in our suffering, we can ask for more peace and more joy and more faith and more hope and more wisdom—and we can trust that a fiercely tender God is holding us together and working these wonders in our souls to "bring us into blossom."

nineteen

REST

*I*n 1858, John Paton and his wife, Mary Ann, went to live with cannibals on an island in the South Seas, compelled by their deep desire to share the love of Christ with those who had never heard His name. However, shortly after arriving on the island, Mary Ann died of pneumonia and malaria. Just three weeks later, the Patons' newborn followed her to the grave. Despite being wrecked by grief and depression, John remained on the island, enduring years of loneliness, ill health, sleepless nights, and constant threats to his own life. Suffering (both emotional and physical) was the price Paton was willing to pay in order to love others.

As I've read and reread Paton's story over the years, I'm struck by how his physical life was marked by such volatility and unrest. Yet Paton understood a *deep rest* that could not be interrupted by illness, grief, death, or danger. He wrote, "I knew not, for one brief hour, when or how attack [against my life] might be made; and yet, with my trembling hand clasped in the hand once nailed on Calvary, and now swaying the sceptre of the universe, calmness and peace and resignation abode in my soul."[1]

Once, when islanders were trying to kill Paton, he ran for his life and hid in a tree overnight. Afterward he wrote,

The hours I spent there live all before me as if it were but of yesterday. I heard the frequent discharging of muskets, and the yells of savages. Yet I sat there among the branches, as safe in the arms of Jesus. Never, in all my sorrows, did my Lord draw nearer to me, and speak more soothingly in my soul, than when the moonlight flickered among these chestnut leaves, and the night air played on my throbbing brow, as I told all my heart to Jesus. . . . If it be to glorify my God, I will not grudge to spend many nights alone in such a tree, to feel again my Savior's spiritual presence, to enjoy his consoling fellowship.[2]

Rhythms of rest are incredibly important to sustain us for the long-term. I've had to work hard at these rhythms over the years: practicing a weekly day of rest, breathing slowly and deeply, taking a quiet walk, observing an earlier bedtime, decluttering my calendar. But Paton's example reminds me that when those rhythms are disrupted by suffering and circumstances outside my control, my perfect resting place remains. The psalmist knew the reality of this when he wrote:

The ropes of death were wrapped around me,
and the torments of Sheol overcame me;
I encountered trouble and sorrow.
Then I called on the name of the LORD,
"LORD, save me!"
The LORD is gracious and righteous;
our God is compassionate.
The LORD guards the inexperienced;
I was helpless, and he saved me.
Return to your rest, my soul,
for the LORD has been good to you.
Pg. 116:3-7

Look how the psalmist moved from overwhelming torments to a state of soul-rest:

He was honest with the Lord ("torments overcame me");

He called on the name of the Lord ("Lord, save me!");

He reminded himself of who God is ("The Lord is gracious . . . compassionate");

He admitted his weakness ("inexperienced," "I was helpless");

He remembered God's salvation ("He saved me"); and

He told his soul to rest, *based on the fact* that God had been good to him.

You may be reading this in a state of intense exhaustion, grief, or anxiety because your burdens feel almost unbearable right now. You are not alone, dear one. You are in good company. Using the model the psalmist gave us, consider spending a few minutes today coaching your soul back to rest in God.

God, today I feel overwhelmed by _____.

So I call on Your name and ask You to save me from

_____.

I want to remember that You are compassionate and _____ [another quality you cherish about God].

But I feel so weak and helpless and _____.
I need You so much, right now, in this very moment.

I thank You that You have saved me from my sin and
the eternal death I deserved! I praise You for rescuing
me from my biggest problem and worst circumstances
imaginable—and making me Your beloved child!

And now I'm telling my soul to rest again because You've
been good to me—not only in saving me and making
me Your own, but also in _____ [recall
another way you've seen God's kindness in your life].

Thank You, God, for showing me how to rest in the
midst of my suffering, how to rest "as safe in the arms of
Jesus." Amen.

twenty

STEP

*T*he Christmas I was twenty-five, I worked in gift-wrapping at a large department store. I'd just left my dream job on the East Coast due to health complications—and I'd returned home to California to heal and piece together a Plan-D life. (Plans B and C are stories for another day.) I ended up substitute teaching at a local high school . . . and wrapping Christmas gifts for stressed and grumpy customers. In my sudden move back home, I'd also left behind my good (paid-in-full) Chevy Corsica, so a dilapidated jalopy became my means of transportation.

It was the perfect recipe for another bout of depression, and those weeks and months were unusually long and dark.

I remember telling myself when I woke up each morning, "Okay, sit up and put your feet on the floor. Now go brush your teeth. Okay, breakfast. Get downstairs and eat."

One foot in front of the other. Take the next step.

As I wrapped Christmas gifts with my son this week, I smiled when he asked me to teach him the tricks of the trade. I thought back on that suffering season twenty years ago and how I never could have fathomed the suffering season we'd be in now—as well as the delight it would bring me to wrap beautiful presents for my family and to teach my son gift-wrapping skills before I'm gone.

That twenty-five-year-old version of me desperately needed just such a seismic shift to my paradigm. Gone were the last vestiges of idealism and naïveté as I watched my health, my dream job, my car, my independence, and my pride shipwreck on the shores of disappointment. But a new beauty was being birthed in me, a new power and resolve that would continue to grow exponentially in the coming years. Richard Baxter's words eloquently describe this transformative time in my life:

Christ leads me through no darker rooms
Than he went through before,
And he that to God's kingdom comes
Must enter by this door.[1]

Baxter was a Puritan preacher whose life was volatile and filled with danger and death, including a prison sentence for his noncompliance with an exploitative government, and the loss of his beloved wife, which he referred to as "a melting grief."[2] Baxter knew what it was to walk through dark places—but to do so with a Guide who knew the way.

I thank God for the raw suffering of 2001. He was opening a door for me into darker rooms so that I would learn to grasp more tightly to His hand and trust Him to lead me into the unknown. He was fleshing out the truth of Isaiah 50:10—

Who among you walks in darkness,
and has no light?
Let him trust in the name of the LORD;
let him lean on his God.

If there's not light for your journey today—if every foot forward feels darker than the one before—take another small step with the One who knows your way. He loves you beyond all telling, and He will fiercely and tenderly lead you through no darker room than He's gone before.

twenty-one

COMPARE

*E*arly this morning, while it was still dark and quiet, I lay in bed and thought about friends who have health and a full head of hair, financial security and energy for ministry, older kids and longer marriages—and I said to God, "It's not fair."

Dangerous words, those.

When I was single in my late twenties and early thirties, my social circles consisted of friends who had married young and popped out beautiful, healthy babies, one right after another. I remember how easy it was back then to think, *It's not fair*. But I learned that those three little words were a sneaky invitation to an epic pity party—and *that* party never ends well. (Think drunken envy and emotional hangovers.) So as quickly as I spoke those words this morning, I wanted to rescind them. Instead, I replaced them with a well-worn prayer: *God, help me see from Your perspective, through Your eyes. Don't let me compare my sufferings with others. Help me trust that You know what's best—and that You love me.*

I reminded myself that not everything is as it seems this moment. In fact, *I see dimly* (1 Cor. 13:12). My ideas of "fairness" are contorted by this blurred, finite vision of mine. I must stop looking all around me and instead look *up* using my "faith vision."

I love Elisabeth Elliot's wisdom in this regard. She wrote,

It depends on our willingness to see everything in God, receive all from His hand, accept with gratitude just the portion and the cup He offers. Shall I charge Him with a mistake in His measurements or with misjudging the sphere in which I can best learn to trust Him? Has He misplaced me? . . . The secret is *Christ* in me, not me in a different set of circumstances. . . . We can only know that Eternal Love is wiser than we, and we bow in adoration of that loving wisdom.[1]

Can I "accept with gratitude" the portion God has given me—or am I "charging Him with a mistake in His measurements"? Do I demand that everyone's portion be equal and identical to mine? Is God loving only if He appears to be "fair"? I remember the apostle Peter's struggle with this. In John 21, we find Peter walking with Jesus, discussing Peter's death of all things. Peter then pointed to John, who was walking behind them, and asked Jesus, "Lord, what about him?"

"If I want him to remain until I come," Jesus answered, "what is that to you? As for you, follow me" (John 21:21–22).

Peter was going to suffer a cruel death, and John was going to long outlive him. But both would know great affliction and pain, both would glorify Jesus through their unique sufferings—and both would be integral to the birth and continued growth of the church.

I love the perspective of time. When I was single and aching to be married with children like my friends, I could not yet see the many ways we would *all* suffer—and the privilege, even the joy, it would be to *suffer together as we followed Jesus* (as we compared ourselves to Him, not to each other). My dearest friends have endured hardships I could not have. And as they've endured those hardships by faith in Christ, I've been encouraged to endure my own hardships with greater strength and joy. I've come to know and love Jesus more because of the way I've seen Him through my friends' sufferings. I am part of a precious "fellowship of sufferers," and in this fellowship, there's no room for elevating one friend's suffering above another's. Instead, we listen to each other, cry with each other, pray like crazy for one another, and laugh together.

So here is my strong encouragement today—for myself and for you: Don't look left. Don't look right. *Look straight ahead and follow Jesus.* Compare yourself to *Him,* to the example He gave us in His death: "For the joy that lay before him, he endured the cross" (Heb. 12:2).

God knows what He is doing, and He knows we need to stay in relationship with a few life-giving friends, even when our pain threatens to build a chasm between us. Maybe no one in your life can fully understand what you're going through right now; maybe others' lives truly are "easier" in some respects—or shockingly "normal." *But we see dimly, and He sees perfectly*—and He is not cheating you while blessing them. He knows what He is doing, and He is pouring out His goodness on you today, even in these (humanly speaking) worst of circumstances. And there is joy waiting on the other side of this cross.

Dear sufferer, let me quickly add this: If today you do speak those three little words, "It's not fair"—out of a heart that hurts because others have what you deeply long for—*He is gentle with you in your weakness and pain.* He will draw you into His loving embrace and hold you and help you. And He will give you the eyes to see from His perspective again. He's fiercely tender like that.

twenty-two

WANT

*E*lisabeth Elliot defined suffering as "having what you don't want and wanting what you don't have."[1] If you're like me, you could come up with a long list of your wants and don't-wants. Life doesn't look at all like we'd imagined it would, does it? Suffering has interrupted our biggest dreams and deepest desires. We want to be happy, but so often we're not.

At the turn of the seventeenth century, Richard Sibbes explained that the desire for happiness is at the root of everything we do: "Happiness being by all men desirable, the desire of it is naturally engrafted in every man; and is the center of all the searchings of his heart and turnings of his life."[2] *All the searchings of our heart and turnings of our life.* It's true. How much time and energy have we expended in the pursuit of happiness?

We try to avoid misery at all costs. We bend over backward to ensure our safety, security, and comfort. We're shocked and angry when bad things happen to us. That's why I love looking through the eyes of saints past, those who lived outside my first-world, entitled American culture. I'm strengthened by reading people like Edward Payson, an eighteenth-century pastor who suffered from depression and a host of physical maladies, including eventual paralysis, yet wrote words like this:

> Christians might avoid much trouble and inconvenience, if they would only believe what they profess: that God is able to make them happy without anything else. . . . To mention my own case—God has been depriving me of one blessing after another; but as every one was removed, he has come in and filled up the place; and now, when I am a cripple, and not able to move, I am happier than I was in all my life before.[3]

How could someone experience *more* happiness after losing all the best things this life has to offer? In his crippled state, Payson said that God alone had made him happier than ever. Payson was echoing what Augustine wrote seventeen centuries before him: "This is the happy life, and this alone: to rejoice in you, about you and because of you. This is the life of happiness, and it is not to be found anywhere else. Whoever thinks there can be some other is chasing a joy that is not the true one."[4]

Suffering is a gift because it strips away our substitute happinesses, chips away at our anemic and worldly wants, and allows us to find indestructible happiness in God. And when we are happy in God, we're freer to enjoy the good things He gives us in this life—because we're no longer *dependent* upon them for our happiness. Our hope is in *God,* not in good stuff or favorable circumstances. As Psalm 146:5 says, "Happy is the one whose help is the God of Jacob, whose hope is in the LORD his God."

When life is humming along uninterrupted by pain or sorrow, we don't feel the need to hope in God or seek His help. But when suffering comes, we find ourselves running to God, crying out for His help, realizing He is our only hope. This running to Him means we're running into the Happiness we so desperately crave. Once again, in the hands of a fiercely tender God, suffering becomes a gift—it's the way to more of Him, the way to truly be happy.

God, our suffering has made us weary and sad—these burdens are so heavy. But we want to be happy in You. Help us run to You again today. Help us seek our help and hope in You so we can find "all the searchings of our heart" satisfied in You. Amen.

twenty-three

TELL

*T*he *Tale of Despereaux* is the story of a brave little mouse who falls in love with a princess and risks his life to save her. Diminutive Despereaux is a story-lover and a storyteller, and he's exiled from his mouse community because he refuses to cower and to give up books and to hate humans. Upon his exile, he ends up in the hands of a miserable mouse-killer named Gregory—but to Despereaux's great surprise, Gregory decides to save him. The dialogue that follows is one of my favorite moments in the book:

"Why would you save me?" Despereaux asked. "Have you saved any of the other mice?"

"Never," said Gregory, "not one."

"Why would you save me, then?"

"Because you, mouse, can tell Gregory a story. Stories are light. Light is precious in a world so dark. Begin at the beginning. Tell Gregory a story. Make some light."[1]

As an English teacher, I began many of my classes perched on a barstool, reading from a chapter book to spellbound teens. No matter how hard the day had been (for them or for me), those moments disarmed and enchanted us all. Enjoying a story together provided us with a common language, a shared experience. It brought a hush over the raucous room and prepared us to tackle the technical lessons that followed.

Years later, when I became a mother, I began curating a list of great stories and books to read to my son. When Jeremy was six months old and struggling to quiet down for naps, I sat in the doorway of his bedroom and read aloud *Around the World in Eighty Days*. We had shelves and piles of picture books, storybooks, and chapter books. We listened to countless audiobooks, and I told Jeremy stories from my childhood (like the time in first grade when I fell off the monkey bars and spontaneously wet my pants and thought I would never live down the mortification)—as well as stories about friends who did fascinating things (like when Karen worked at the White House and high-fived the king of Jordan when he visited).

We are made for stories. After all, we are made in God's image, and He is the greatest storyteller of all time. His Book is one big, beautiful love story, from Genesis to Revelation. It's full of mystery and intrigue and suffering and redemption—all pointing to the main character, Jesus (who also told stories when He was on earth, to reveal His heart and His kingdom).

Stories are especially precious and powerful when life is dark. Like Gregory said, stories are light in a dark world. In times of suffering, I've found that telling a loved one a story—whether it's bound in a book or drawn from my memory—helps dispel the darkness. It quiets the tumult. It reconnects us relationally (especially if there's been division between us). It gives us a common vocabulary for our pain. It gently paves our way back to Hope.

What story do you know that is hopeful and kind? Beautiful and redemptive? Inspiring or hilarious? Maybe it's your favorite book or a happy memory or a story your grandmother told you long ago. Maybe it's a time when you experienced God's goodness in your suffering or someone else's kindness in your pain. Perhaps today is a good day to tell your story to someone you love—and shine some light into the darkness.[2]

twenty-four

LEAN

What's been the most surprising part of this journey?"
How would *you* answer that? Someone posed this
question to me today and I surprised myself with how quickly
I answered, "How indescribably *awful* some moments are—
especially in light of how much our family has already been
through. But then I'm equally surprised that, as horrible as
those moments are, they always pass—and joy comes again."

I went on to explain that in those bewilderingly painful
moments, I'm at a complete loss for words. Typically all I
can pray is a desperate, "God, help us. Please, *please help us.*"
Yesterday afternoon found me praying this again as our little family of three seemed to be unraveling before my very

eyes. I wondered how we would make it to the other side of such moments. All our intense needs and pains were surfacing again and crashing into one another. And as we muddled through it all, sloppy in our suffering, I took long deep breaths and stared out the window, silently begging God to help us.

In his inimitable book, *Weakness Is the Way,* J. I. Packer wrote,

> The truth . . . is that in many respects, and certainly in spiritual matters, we are all weak and inadequate, and we need to face it. Sin, which disrupts all relationships, has disabled us all across the board. We need to be aware of our limitations and to let this awareness work in us humility and self-distrust, and a realization of our helplessness on our own. Thus we may learn our need to depend on Christ, our Savior and Lord, at every turn of the road, to practice that dependence as one of the constant habits of our hearts, and hereby to discover what Paul discovered before us: "when I am weak, then I am strong" (2 Cor. 12:10).[1]

Suffering provokes our weakness, amplifies it, exposes it in all its ugliness. Take me to dinner at a cliffside restaurant with a sunset view, and I will be the picture of perfection. But drop me in the middle of the ocean without a lifejacket, and I will be a far less admirable version of myself.

But in exposing our weakness (weakness that was already there, mind you), suffering does us a great favor: it helps us feel the tragic depths of our fragility, which sends us running into Strength itself—and Strength transforms us, making us look a wee bit more like Him today than we did yesterday. When people say I'm the strongest person they know, I laugh. I'm absolutely the weakest person I know, and I could produce plenty of proof to convince you of it. But I've spent so many years leaning hard into God's power (asking Him to be for me what I cannot be for myself) that to the untrained eye *His* strength in me can be mistaken for my own. He is in me, and I am in Him, and so my weakness doesn't have the final say—His strength does.

But still, I feel every inch of my frailty. I write this book out of breathtaking weakness, and I do so with the prayer that others who feel weak—others who also fear that their suffering might be their undoing—will be able to look up at Strength and say with me, in the words of the psalmist,

As my strength fails, do not abandon me. . . .
God, do not abandon me,
while I proclaim your power

to another generation,
your strength to all who are to come. . . .
You who have done great things;
God, who is like you?
You caused me to experience
many troubles and misfortunes,
but you will revive me again.
You will bring me up again,
even from the depths of the earth. . . .
My lips will shout for joy. . . .
I will hope continually
And will praise you more and more.
Ps. 71:9, 18–20, 23, 14

Yes, yesterday held some indescribably awful moments, but as I leaned hard into God, He heard my cry for help, and He revived me—He revived *us*—again. Our family ended the day making the sweetest memories and enjoying each other's company, which was not something we could have manufactured on our own. It was a gift from God, whose power brings us up again (and again and again), "even from the depths of the earth" (see Ps. 71:20).

Dear sufferer, what feels indescribably awful to you right now? Is it the long, relentless fight for sexual abstinence?

A deeply wounded relationship? A devastating diagnosis? Whatever it may be, don't resent feeling the depths of your weakness in it. The awful moments inevitably expose the mess in us, but the mess is an invitation to lean into Him who is with us in all His power. *The leaning is liberating.* It frees us from our miserable self-reliance and puts us into the arms of Love.

Lean into Him. Lean hard. He wants to be fiercely tender for you again today.

twenty-five

LISTEN

I've been told to eat more blueberries, sit in the sun till I'm red as a lobster, use essential oils and flaxseed enemas, think loving thoughts, stop all medications, and "just find a doctor who uses vegetables"—to cure my stage-four cancer. (And that's the abbreviated list to be sure.) Without knowing how clean I already eat or how chemical-free our family lives or how many natural health protocols I practice daily, many well-intentioned people have told me what to do and how to do it—and assured me that God would heal me as a result.

Believe me, I hate chemotherapy as much as the next person does. And years ago I turned my back on microwaves and aluminum deodorants and sugary, processed foods. The way

I cook and eat could qualify as an Olympic event. I've done infrared saunas and coffee enemas and colon hydrotherapy and vitamin C IVs. I absolutely get why people are strong proponents of natural methods. And I also understand why they speak up: over the years, out of a desire to help others, I've dished out my fair share of hasty and ill-informed advice. It's why I won't be offended tomorrow when someone tells me I can cure my cancer if I just "juice more kale."

But it's not just cancer that elicits loud voices and strong opinions. If you are sick, skinny, not-so-skinny, infertile, dating, divorced, unemployed, or unattached (need I go on?), you've most likely been the recipient of shockingly misguided advice. There's always so much more to our suffering and our circumstances than the casual observer understands, right? We can't control what others say, but we *can* tune our hearts to listen all the more carefully to the One Voice who speaks perfect words of wisdom, who never sticks His foot in His mouth, who always knows exactly what to say and when to say it. I have long loved Psalm 12:6 for this reason—

The words of the LORD are pure words,
like silver refined in an earthen furnace,
purified seven times.

And Psalm 29 says,

> *The voice of the LORD is above the waters.*
> *The God of glory thunders—*
> *the LORD, above the vast water,*
> *the voice of the LORD in power,*
> *the voice of the LORD in splendor. . . .*
> *The voice of the LORD flashes flames of fire.*
> *The voice of the LORD shakes the wilderness.*
> *Ps.* 29:3–4, 7–8

I cringe to think of the countless words I have spoken to others that have been so far from pure and refined. And my voice has never thundered or thrown flames or caused an earthquake.

But *His* has. *His* does.

There is no sweeter or stronger voice than His. He has perfect words for us in our suffering. Even better, the apostle John tells us He *is* the Word. The Word who created us. The Word who is our life. The Word who is our light—light that the darkness cannot overcome (John 1:1–5)!

He is the One Word we need for life itself. When He speaks, He sustains us, strengthens us, satisfies us. There is no better word than His.

But wait. If God's voice is the only one that speaks perfect words—and the rest of us speak incredibly *imperfect* words—does this mean we don't need to listen to each other? Does this give us permission to blow off other people's counsel? *Quite the contrary.* God often uses wise and seasoned saints to help us hear Him more clearly. That's why this book is filled with wisdom from those who have gone before us, and that's why I stay deeply connected to my inner circle of friends and family and spiritual leaders. As we tune our hearts to listen for God, He will often use "a multitude of counselors" (Prov. 15:22 NKJV) to speak to us. He will use a friend's words to give us courage when we are fearful. He will use a pastor's sermon to renew our hope. He will use an old saint's writings to shine light into a dark day.

But we listen to Him *first and last and above all others*. His words "are not meaningless words to you but *they are your life*" (Deut. 32:47).

Next time someone tells you how to find a husband within two business days or how to heal yourself with a magic elixir or how to fix your prodigal child in three easy steps—cover their ignorant words with love (even as you and I want to be loved every time we say something stupid). Then go back to the perfect, life-giving, light-emanating Word and listen to Him as He speaks tenderly and truthfully into your deepest need.

So now, Lord, every day—sometimes every hour—when I hear your voice, I have to cry out, "No one ever spoke like this man!" (John 7:46). Your words are sweet and perfect for my weary soul, and my sense of nothingness makes your fullness even more precious.

Be all I need, dearest Lord. Let me hear your voice and see your countenance. Because both in life and in death, in time and to all eternity, the voice of my Lord Jesus will be my everlasting comfort.

No one speaks like you! Amen.[1]

twenty-six

NUMBER

hen a strong and handsome man named Eddie Chao asked me to marry him twelve years ago—at the foot of a white cross on a hill overlooking the ocean—a thrilling countdown began. With a sparkly diamond ring on my finger, I was ecstatic to tick off the 123 days till I became Mrs. Eddie Chao.

When a doctor informed me a year ago of a very different kind of countdown—telling me my days on earth were numbered—I responded quite differently. When no one was around, I wept, I wailed, I curled up in my closet in the fetal position, I lost my appetite and my sleep.

No, it wasn't my first rodeo with cancer; it wasn't even the first time I'd come face to face with my mortality; rather, it was the cold, hard fact that Death was at my doorstep to take me from my loved ones. That's what wrecked me.

But why all the angst over the inevitable? Why mourn over the promise of seeing my First Love sooner than later? Isn't that all my hope and longing and glory? I *want* to go home! I can't wait to be face to face with Jesus! So why was I grieving so hard? Perhaps for the very first time, I truly understood the apostle Paul's struggle in Philippians 1:

> For me, to live is Christ and to die is gain. Now if I live on in the flesh, this means fruitful work for me; and I don't know which one I should choose. *I am torn between the two.* I long to depart and be with Christ—which is far better—but to remain in the flesh is more necessary for your sake.
> Phil. 1:21–24

Even as this Scripture came alive in a new way, I knew I also needed someone to model for me how to walk through this valley of the shadow of death with grace and grit. With hope and purpose. A man named Lemuel Haynes helped show me the way.

Haynes was familiar with death and loss: he was abandoned by his mother and indentured to a family when he was just a baby. During his youth he had multiple scrapes with death and, during his tenure as a pastor, he preached more than 520 funerals.[1] Death was a daily reality for him. He wrote,

> Neither prosperity nor adversity will much affect him who expects every hour to come to the end of his journey or close his eyes on things below. . . . Were it constantly sounding in our ears, "The time of my departure is at hand!," it would have a salutary [favorable, healing] influence on our conduct, and others would derive unspeakable advantage from it.[2]

Those were the words I needed! To know that death is near can actually be *healing* and *helpful* to us, favorably affecting the way we live our lives. Instead of grasping for eternal youth and health and beauty, we embrace the reality that our lives are:

short-lived,

just inches long,

a vanishing vapor,

a breath,

a passing shadow, and

flowers that wither.

(Pss. 39:4–5, 11; 144:4; Job 7:7; Isa. 40:7–8; James 4:14)

One of the bittersweet blessings of suffering is the way it moves us a little closer to our infinite reality. It doesn't have to be a terminal diagnosis. You may be watching your career crumble, a relationship unravel, or your parent suffer from dementia. Affliction of any kind can help pry our little-kid fingers off our little-earth treasures so we have open hands to receive indestructibly good gifts from God. Suddenly we care less about preserving our bodies and perfecting our financial portfolio and being *right* all the time. Instead, we find ourselves thinking bigger thoughts, longing for what lasts, and praying with Moses, "Teach us to number our days carefully so that we may develop wisdom in our hearts" (Ps. 90:12).

When we view our life here on earth as long and secure, we easily settle for lesser loves and substitute comforts. But when we hurt and yearn and grieve, when the pain won't go away—head knowledge of our mortality becomes heart wisdom, and we begin to see past the human carnival of cheap thrills and into the pleasures of God's forever kingdom.

Paul said that death is gain, and Moses said that thinking about our impending death puts wisdom in our hearts. It's not morbid to take these wise men's advice and think often about how brief this life is. Whether we live twenty years or ninety, our time here is just a few inches long. What hope that is for the sufferer! Our suffering is granting us wisdom and accumulating eternal reward; it's giving us more of Jesus; it's equipping us with comfort to pass along to others—*but our suffering won't last forever.* Thank You, God! It will be over before we know it, and it will be replaced by gorgeous, weighty, eternal glory.

Whatever our suffering today, let it compel us to follow in the footsteps of Paul and Moses and Lemuel and thousands of others who have gone before us to show us the way of wisdom. Let us echo their cry: *Lord, help us to number our days!*

twenty-seven

HOPE

*I*n the early mornings, I lie in bed and listen through the Psalms on my audio Bible. As I listen, I pray. (I love that Scripture gives us words to pray when we don't have any.) Recently Psalm 71 has captured my heart, and I've prayed often through its verses, including:

> *Be a rock of refuge for me, where I can always go.*
>
> *I have leaned on you from birth; you took me from my mother's womb.*
>
> *As my strength fails, do not abandon me.*
>
> *My praise is always about you. . . . I still proclaim your wondrous works.*

As I've continued praying through this psalm, one verse in particular feels like the hinge my hearts swings on:

For you are my hope, Lord GOD.
v. 5

God doesn't just *give* me hope—He *is* my Hope.

This verse has encouraged me so much that today I dug a little deeper into it. I looked up this specific Hebrew word for "hope," and what I discovered made my heart soar: the Hebrew word, *tiqvâ*, is translated first as "cord," then as "hope, expectation, outcome." I was almost giddy as I dug even deeper and found that *tiqvâ* is "literally a cord (as an attachment); figuratively, expectancy."[1] Then I looked up where and how the word is used elsewhere in Scripture. The first place listed was Joshua 2—the account of the Israelite spies and the prostitute Rahab. Rahab spared the spies from death and then asked them to spare her from death in return. The spies answered her,

"We will give our lives for yours. If you don't report our mission, we will show kindness and faithfulness to you when the LORD gives us the land. . . .

". . . when we enter the land, you tie this scarlet cord [tiqvâ] to the window through which you let us down." . . .

"Let it be as you say," she replied, and she sent them away. After they had gone, she tied the scarlet cord [tiqvâ] *to the window.* Josh. 2:14, 18, 21

What did this *tiqvâ*, this cord, represent? *It represented Rahab's hope*—the hope of being rescued, the hope of saving her family from death, the hope of God's people showing her kindness and faithfulness.

No one could have guessed that after tying that scarlet cord to her window and being rescued from death, Rahab would eventually marry an Israelite man named Salmon, and they would have a son named Boaz; and Boaz and his wife, Ruth, would have a son named Obed; and Obed would have a son named Jesse, and Jesse would have a son named David. And many generations later, a descendant of David would be born, and His name would be Jesus. Rahab, once a prostitute and an enemy of God, hung a scarlet *hope* in her window, and her story became inextricably tied up with that of the Savior, the Hope of the world.

Today I too hang my *tiqvâ* through the window of my threatening circumstances and say, *God, You don't just give me hope—You* are *my Hope. You will rescue me. You will redeem this suffering. You will show Your kindness and faithfulness once again. Thank You that I can wholly trust You. Amen.*

twenty-eight

DANCE

*A*fter a week of navigating more of chemo's rigorous side effects and layers of physical pain, getting a molar extracted due to an infection in my gums, shaving my head down to the nubs (again), missing my son's back-to-school activities, and postponing our anniversary dinner because I was too sick to get out—there's a not-so-sneaky temptation to despair, to nurse longings for "normalcy," or to live in sheer *survival mode.*

But at the beginning of this new week, I'm looking over my shoulder and I can clearly see that a strong and gentle King saw me in my weepy heap of weariness, pushed through the masses to get to me, took my hand, drew me close, and slowly danced with me through the week, speaking words of hope and promise and goodness to me. All week long He has been with me. All week long He has had merciful words to sing over me.

On Saturday He sang Psalm 55:16 over me, reminding me that He loves to save His children. It's what He does. "How he will save me I cannot guess; but he will do it, I know."[1] My heart grew ten times bigger to remember that He will not give me over to despair and darkness and a grievous end. That's not what He does. Even though cancer most likely will take me, *He will rescue me from this affliction in His perfect way,* and it will mean life and joy and freedom for many others, not just me.

Midweek He was singing over me truths from the Gospels as I meditated on Jesus' ministry on earth, specifically the throngs who came from miles around to touch Him and be healed. These were people who had suffered horrifically for years and even decades, some with terminal illnesses, some with incurable diseases, some with pain that kept them up every night, some with disabilities that brought about their destitution. But when they heard about the Miraculous Healing Man, they pushed through every pain and limitation to get to Him, desperate as they were for relief and wholeness and normalcy, for freedom from social stigmas, for the hope of becoming functioning members of their families and community again.

And Jesus healed them. He had compassion on them.

Which raises the question: Is this Jesus who healed the multitudes two thousand years ago the same Jesus who may choose *not* to heal *me*, His beloved daughter? Will the Jesus who showed compassion to the crowds allow a young boy to watch his mom slowly waste away—then grow up without her? Allow a husband to lose his wife and find himself a single dad?

Even while Jesus was showing the world what His kingdom would look like—*Healing! Restoration! Power over dark forces! Forgiveness of sins!*—He was promising His followers that they would suffer greatly. *That* would be the way His kingdom would fully come—through faith-filled, joyful, suffering saints. It wasn't comfort and security and ease He was selling.

He came in this beautiful juxtaposition: both to introduce us to His breathtakingly good kingdom by mending broken people, *and* to be the suffering servant who knows agony in all of its layers and grief in all of its stages. This way we would learn how to suffer in His footsteps, dance in step with Him—and the world would look at us and marvel, "They have more joy and more peace and more purpose in their suffering than I have on my best days of ease and security. What's their secret?!" More people would be forgiven and freed and swallowed up in joy, and the kingdom would grow and grow until one day King Jesus brings it in all its fullness, and we see

> *a new heaven and a new earth; for the first heaven and the first earth had passed away, and the sea was no more. I also saw the holy city, the new Jerusalem, coming down out of heaven from God, prepared like a bride adorned for her husband.*
>
> *Then I heard a loud voice from the throne: Look, God's dwelling is with humanity, and he will live with them. They will be his peoples, and God himself will be with them and will be their God. He will wipe away every tear from their eyes. Death will be no more; grief, crying, and pain will be no more, because the previous things have passed away.*
>
> *Then the one seated on the throne said, "Look, I am making everything new."*
> Rev. 21:1-5

Wouldn't you just love to opt out of the suffering and skip to the good stuff of Revelation 21? I'm constantly and keenly aware of how soft I am. I think of the many biographies I've read of saints past who suffered unthinkable losses and crosses (and didn't whine but counted it a joy and privilege). I think of our brothers and sisters around the world today who are choosing to remain in hostile places, risking life and limb and loved ones in order to share the good news of Jesus with people who have never heard His name. I look at my own insidious bent toward first-world comforts and securities and expectations, and I cry out to God to increase my capacity to suffer well, with more and more joy, to toughen me up while keeping me tender, and to help me relinquish the treasures I have on this earth (which oh-so-quickly become idols in my heart).

I'm so grateful for God's gentleness with me. He is happy to be with me in my weakness, and He will finish the good work He started in me. He is patiently teaching me how to look death in the face and say,

Time, how short!
Death, how brief!
Eternity, how long!
Immortality, how endless![2]

And so today, because He takes me into His arms and dances with me in a crowded room of sorrows, I can take up this cross again, deny myself, and follow Him down a path I never would have chosen—but a path that leads to *eternal pleasures.*[3]

twenty-nine

UNDERSTAND

The kingdom of God works backward. Jesus told us to love our enemies and bless those who persecute us. He said we find our life when we lose it. He promised that the last will be first, and the first last—and the greatest person among us will be the humblest servant.

And so it is with suffering.

What looks like the end of all hope is its very dawning. What feels like the deepest, darkest pit is really a sacred entrance into more of Christ. Our heartaches today are the labor pains before fierce joy is born. This is God's way—a hard but beautiful way—and we sufferers often struggle to perceive and embrace it.

One of my favorite books of all time is C. S. Lewis's *The Great Divorce*. In it he writes of a man who sees himself both in heaven and in hell, and at one point a wise guide explains to him the eternal reality this way:

"Son," he said, "ye cannot in your present state understand eternity. . . . But ye can get some likeness of it if ye say that both good and evil, when they are full grown, become retrospective. Not only this valley but all their earthly past will have been Heaven to those who are saved. . . . That is what mortals misunderstand. They say of some temporal suffering, 'No future bliss can make up for it,' not knowing that Heaven, once attained, will work backwards and turn even that agony into a glory. And of some sinful pleasure they say 'Let me have but this and I'll take the consequences': little dreaming how damnation will spread back and back into their past and contaminate the pleasure of the sin. Both processes begin even before death. The good man's past begins to change so that his forgiven sins and remembered sorrows take on the quality of Heaven: the bad man's past already conforms to his badness and is filled only with dreariness. And that is why, at the end of all things, when the sun rises here and the twilight turns to blackness down there, the Blessed will say 'We have never lived anywhere except in Heaven,' and the Lost, 'We were always in Hell.' And both will speak truly."[1]

Lewis's idea was not a new one—the apostle Paul wrote of this hope-filled reality a couple thousand years before:

For our momentary light affliction is producing for us an absolutely incomparable eternal weight of glory. So we do not focus on what is seen, but on what is unseen. For what is seen is temporary, but what is unseen is eternal.
2 Cor. 4:17–18

Today, let's look past the quickly fading reality of this temporary existence—and fix our eyes instead on the solid reality of heaven. Heaven works backward. And one day soon it will turn all this momentary agony into infinite glory.

thirty

ANTICIPATE

As soon as my son could carry on a simple conversation, I talked often with him about eternity. I read Scriptures to him describing what the new heavens and the new earth will be like. I marveled with him at the descriptions of Jesus in John's Revelation. I stopped to discuss C. S. Lewis's imagery of heaven when we read (and reread) his book *The Last Battle.* We chatted about our eternal home as if it were just next door. And as we did, I was constantly astounded to hear a little boy process fathomless realities with childlike faith and insights.

Then cancer came. Jeremy was only six years old when I was first diagnosed. That's a lot for a little guy to take in, but at the same time—wasn't this a natural progression of our many conversations about eternity? Heaven was just moving in a bit closer.

Then, a year ago, when we found out that my cancer had returned and was now terminal, Jeremy (nine years old) lay in bed next to me and wept, "I don't want you to die, Mom," and "Why did God let you get cancer a second time?"

Those are sacred parenting moments. Moments so painful yet so utterly precious, you can almost feel God's breath on you as you gently walk your child through grief to hope, reminding him of what you so desperately need to remember yourself: *This is not our home.* No, home is where . . .

> *God's dwelling is with humanity, and he will live with them. They will be his peoples, and God himself will be with them and will be their God. He will wipe away every tear from their eyes. Death will be no more; grief, crying, and pain will be no more, because the previous things have passed away.*
> Rev. 21:3–4

Home is where He is, and because He is there, every good desire is fulfilled, every beautiful dream comes true, every breathtaking wonder is realized. Home is where we finally get to be perfectly happy and healthy and whole.

These days our family lives on the razor's edge. Death is our ever-present reality. Brevity is our new normal. I am inches away from the realities we've talked of for years. And although I'm longing to be home with my Forever Love, nothing in me wants to prematurely leave my husband and son, leave them behind to grieve and suffer after *my* suffering is done. I want to stay here and love them longer and shelter them from such pain.

But the reality is, home is breathtakingly close for Eddie and Jeremy too. For a time, suffering may make their days feel long and terrible, but in the end, it will be all the same to us—and we will be in His presence forever and ever and ever.

Years ago, when I taught a high school girls' Bible study, I took a dry-erase marker and drew a tiny dot on a large white board and said, "Imagine that this is the entirety of history, from Creation to the end of time. If that were true, then eternity would be everything beyond this dot, to the far reaches of space."

For a moment, we live in the dot. When Jeremy has another nightmare about me dying, or Eddie sheds silent tears, or I hear another ominous test result—it helps to remember how infinitesimally small our present reality is and how infinitely boundless our eternal home is.

In *The Last Battle*, C. S. Lewis imagines heaven with poignant descriptions and dialogue. In one particular scene, Narnian animals and children are just beginning to understand their new life in gloriously perfected Narnia:

> It was the Unicorn who summed up what everyone was feeling. . . . "I have come home at last! This is my real country! I belong here. This is the land I have been looking for all my life, though I never knew it till now."[1]

Dear sufferer, before we know it, we'll be in "the land we have been looking for all our life." Our pain is passing. We are almost home.

thirty-one

LOVE

C ontrary to what suffering might initially lead us to believe, God has not cheated us. He has always outgiven us, whether we've been able to recognize it or not. I may be staring death in the face, while you may be looking down the gun of a divorce you never wanted—but together we are looking at a life that turned out nothing like we'd hoped it would. Yet that unexpected life is proof that we have been deeply, undeservedly loved.

How can this be? How can suffering persuade us of God's *love*?

In my early twenties, as I read through the book of Ezekiel, I came to a passage that surprised and captivated me. Ezekiel 16 is the story of a kindly king who found a wee babe still covered in her blood and afterbirth—abandoned in an open field and left to die. When the mighty king saw her, he said to her, "Live!" And she did. Not only did he speak life over her, but he also washed her, gave her a lavish wardrobe, fed her the finest foods, placed a crown on her head, and made her breathtakingly beautiful.

I love the story of Ezekiel 16 (an allegory of God's relationship with Israel) because it's my story too: I was born into the deathly condition of sin yet was loved to life by the King. Oh, how I love Him for how He has loved me (1 John 4:19)! He has saved me, made me His own, cleaned me, clothed me, and made me beautiful. Because He has loved me so lavishly, I can trust that whatever affliction He allows in my life flows from love far greater and wiser than my own. I can trust that He will do only what's best for me.

There have been moments, even days and weeks, when I have doubted His love. The suffering feels too cruel, or He seems a million miles away. In the disappointments and depression of my twenties, when I was tempted to wonder at the hand and heart of God, I began mining Scripture for proof of His love—proof that would transcend my circumstances and emotions. Not only did Ezekiel 16 become a lifeline for my soul, but so did many other verses and passages. What I found evolved into a lengthy "love list" that I have revisited often these twenty-five years. I share it with you now in hopes that you will experience ever more of the "length and width, height and depth of God's love" for you (Eph. 3:18).

He leads me with cords of kindness and ropes of love. (Hos. 11:4)

He has engraved me on the palm of His hand. (Isa. 49:16)

He carries me close to His heart. (Isa. 40:11)

He holds my hand. (Ps. 73:23)

He will do abundantly more than all I can ask or imagine. (Eph. 3:20)

He daily bears my burdens. (Ps. 68:19)

He thinks of me constantly: His thoughts of me out-number the grains of sand on the sea. (Ps. 139:17–18)

He gives me life, beauty, and dignity. (Ezek. 16:1–14)

He is intimately interested in my life. He even knows how many hairs are on my head. (Matt. 10:30)

He has planned out my days. (Pss. 139:16; 118:24)

He intercedes for me. (Heb. 7:25; Rom. 8:26)

He freely forgives me. (1 John 1:9; Ps. 103:12)

He rejoices over me like a bridegroom rejoices over his bride. (Isa. 62:5)

He protects and rescues me. (Ps. 91)

He understands my temptations and weaknesses. (Heb. 2:17–18)

He gives me the power to live like Him. (Rom. 8:9–11; Phil. 4:13)

He delights in me and rejoices over me with singing. (Zeph. 3:17)

He teaches me what is best for me. (Isa. 48:17)

He helps me. (Isa. 41:10, 14; Ps. 118:13; Deut. 33:26)

He created me for a special purpose and designed me to be His wonderful creation. (Ps. 139:13–14; Jer. 1:5; Eph. 2:10)

He will fulfill His purpose for me. (Ps. 138:8; Phil. 1:6)

His love for me is as high as the heavens are above the earth. (Ps. 103:11)

He makes my path level and smooth. (Isa. 26:7)

He is always with me. (Ps. 73:23)

He guides me with His counsel. (Ps. 73:24)

He gives me wisdom. (James 1:5)

He keeps record of all my tears. (Ps. 56:8)

He satisfies my hunger and quenches my thirst. (John 6:35)

He leads me and knows me. (John 10:27)

He gives me life to the fullest. (John 10:10)

He laid down His life for me. (John 10:11)

He gives me good and perfect gifts. (James 1:17)

He listens to me; He hears my cry. (Ps. 145:19)

He fulfills my desires. (Pss. 145:19; 37:4)

He has compassion on me. (Ps. 145:9)

He makes me happy. (Pss. 16:11; 36:8)

He has made me His child. (Rom. 8:14; Gal. 4:5; 3:26)

He has given me fullness in Christ, and I am complete. (Col. 2:9–10)

He has given me a home in heaven. (Col. 1:13; Eph. 2:6)

He has lavished on me all the riches of His grace. (Eph. 1:7–8)

He longs to give me His very best. (Isa. 1:19)

He is distressed in my distress. (Isa. 63:9)

He lifts me up and carries me. (Isa. 63:14)

He leads me through the depths and the darkness. (Isa. 50:10)

He directs my steps. (Prov. 20:24)

He chooses to forget my sins; He buries them in the deep sea. (Isa. 43:25; Mic. 7:19)

He has given me an inheritance far beyond my imagination. (Ps. 47:4; Eph. 1:18; Col. 1:12)

He gives me the strength to serve Him. (1 Peter 4:11)

Dear fellow sufferer, you are deeply, infinitely, perfectly loved by the King who made you and caused you to live. Yes, this present suffering may be indescribably hard, but the King loves you too much to spare you from it, for He knows it is the way into more of His love. Corrie ten Boom wrote, "The Lord paid a hefty price to be with us forever and to prove how outrageous His love is. . . . We must always remember that God's love can make us conquerors and set us free if we receive Him with open and trusting hearts."[1]

God, open and enlarge our hearts to experience more of Your love today.

IMAGINE

There once was a king who rode a white horse and carried a sword in his mouth. He led an army of Thor-like warriors, and they followed him into battle with more loyalty and love than any other army had ever followed their king. The king wore a white robe with a blood-red hem. He was so great, and his robe was so immense that he—and it—seemed to fill up every inch of his vast palace. Fantastical creatures covered with eyes and wings hovered above him, constantly declaring how infinitely astonishing he was. Indeed, he was so astonishing that his body glowed like a furnace, his hair was white like snow, his eyes blazed like flames, and his voice thundered. His dwelling place smoked and quaked with his greatness. Everyone who entered his presence trembled, falling to their knees, pressing their faces to the ground.

This incomparably powerful king was also immeasurably good and kind, so no one stayed forever on their face. They stood up and laughed and sang and danced in the king's presence. With his endless wealth (for every last thing belonged to him and no one wanted it any other way), the king built for the citizens of his kingdom breathtakingly beautiful rooms in his palace—rooms so costly and exquisite that not even the wealthiest man in the world today could afford to buy one. The king also prepared and hosted magnificent feasts, the likes of which have never been seen before or since—feasts at long tables overflowing with fine wines and choice foods. No citizen ever missed a feast, for not only was the food divine, but also the king was there—and being in his presence was like being with all the most wonderful people you've ever known rolled into one person, but even better.

Because the king was so good and so kind and so powerful, no one ever got sick. (Not even a sniffle.) And no one was ever in any pain. (Not even a headache.) No one wept or grieved. No one argued or felt even the tiniest impulse of envy or anger or lust or shame. No one ever moved away or died, so friends and family never had to say goodbye to each other on the phone or at the front door or in a graveyard. Boredom and apathy were banished. Fear and anxiety could not be found. No one lacked any good thing. There was perfect happiness and security and unity and peace. Every citizen's dreams were realized in this kingdom, every longing fulfilled.

And, unlike every other king who died and whose kingdom came to an end, this King *was*, still *is*, and always *will be*. His bright and beautiful and bold and happy kingdom goes on and on and on. It lasts forever, and all of His citizens experience greater and greater happiness the longer they are there with Him. If you took the King out of His kingdom, no one would want to stay. For the wonders and joys and feasts and rooms and friendships and beauty flow forever from this King's perfect presence.[1]

— — —

Dear sufferer, this King loves you beyond all telling, and He can't wait to share the vast and breathtaking glories of His kingdom with you. While we are still on this side of things (for just a few more breaths), His kingdom is in our hearts and its beauty is growing stronger in us through our sufferings. With every passing pain, with each new day, we are that much closer to hearing Him say, "Well done, good and faithful servant! You were faithful over a few things; I will put you in charge of many things. Share your master's joy" (Matt. 25:21).

31 DAYS OF THANKSGIVING

When I think upon and converse with thee
Ten thousand delightful thoughts spring up,
Ten thousand sources of pleasure are unsealed,
Ten thousand refreshing joys spread over my heart,
Crowding into every moment . . .[1]

Day 1 _____

_____

Day 2 _____

_____

Day 3 _____

_____

Day 4 _____

_____

Day 5 _____

_____

Day 6 _____

_____

Day 7 _____

_____

Day 8 _____

_____

Day 9 _____

_____

Day 10 _____

_____

Day 11 _____

_____

Day 12 _____

_____

Day 13 _____

_____

Day 14 _____

_____

Day 15 _____

_____

Day 16 _____

_____

Day 17 _____

_____

Day 18 _____

_____

Day 19 _____

_____

Day 20 _____

_____

Day 21 _____

_____

Day 22 _____

_____

Day 23 _____

_____

Day 24 _____

_____

Day 25 _____

_____

Day 26 _____

_____

Day 27 _____

_____

Day 28 _____

_____

Day 29 _____

_____

Day 30 _____

_____

Day 31 _____

_____

ACKNOWLEDGMENTS

This book was grown in the rich soil of countless precious relationships—and these acknowledgments do not do justice to the gratitude I owe so many. Those I mention by name here are the ones who faithfully and sacrificially upheld me and cheered me on during the book-writing process. I am grateful beyond these words—

Kristie Anyabwile: as soon as I told you of my desire to write a book, you opened impossible doors for me. This book is the fruit of your time, wisdom, faith, and friendship.

Pastor Milton and Donna, and my beloved community at Cornerstone Fellowship Bible Church: your wisdom and encouragement have strengthened me to write; your generosity and love will follow me into eternity.

Brooks Buser, Lindsey Carlson, Greg Coles, Erin Davis—you, dear friends, had no time to read another book, yet you made time to read mine, then risked putting your name to it. I'm forever honored and grateful.

My Moody Publishers team (Trillia, Cheryl, Erik, Kelsey, Karen, Eddie, Ashley, Kathryn, Connor, et al.): your faith and vision and expertise turned my heart's vision into reality. What a privilege it has been to work with you all.

Kim Cash Tate: your confidence that God's anointing was on this book gave me courage on days when I had none.

Nancy DeMoss Wolgemuth: you saw God's hand in my story and helped me share that story with many others these past five years. I wrote with greater faith and conviction because of you.

My five "besties" (Nina, Wendi, Lisa, Karen, and Carlynne): I thought of you with every page I wrote—and had to restrain myself from talking about you at every turn. Oh, how I love you five.

My big, beautiful family (Pops, Mommers, David, Heather, Jonathan, Shawna, Katy, Jeff, Chris, Nathan, Aaron, Kylie, Ethan, Caleb, Daniel, Elise, Joshua): I could trace each of you through these pages. Your love for me has shaped me. Thank you for your listening ears, insightful conversations, prayers, fasting, and encouragement as I wrote. I love you all something fierce.

Jeremy: I would have written this book just for you—so that you could hear my voice whisper comfort and guidance as you suffer in the coming days. But you agreed that other sufferers needed this book as well, so you selflessly let me share my heart and my words with them. You are my joy. I love you more than you will ever know.

Eddie: You are the best man I know. You have suffered alongside me and for me and with me, carrying the heaviest burdens with such grace—all while dreaming God's dreams for me and cheering me on as I wrestled through the pages of this book. I wrote from the strength of your lavish love (Songs 8:6–7).

Jesus: my words are shabby things when it comes to describing the exquisite ways I've been loved by You. But You told me to write, and so I've written. I can't wait for the Day when these feeble words become face-to-face reality, and I run into the arms of my Forever Love.

NOTES

Chapter 1: Look

1. Isaac Ambrose, *Looking Unto Jesus: A View of the Everlasting Gospel* (Pittsburgh: L. Loomis, 1832), 8, 9–10.
2. Ibid.

Chapter 2: Remember

1. Jeremiah Burroughs, *The Rare Jewel of Christian Contentment* (London: W. Bentley, 1651), 128. Spelling and capitalization modernized.

Chapter 3: Cry

1. C. H. Spurgeon, *The Silent Shades of Sorrow* (Scotland: Christian Focus Publications, 2015), 61.

Chapter 4: Thank

1. Corrie ten Boom, *God Is My Hiding Place* (Ada, MI: Chosen Books, 2021), 225.
2. Thomas Watson, *All Things for Good* (Shawnee, KS: Gideon House Books, 2015), 55.

Chapter 5: Do

1. Ellen Vaughn, *Becoming Elisabeth Elliot* (Nashville: B&H Publishing Group, 2020), 268.
2. Ibid., 269.

Chapter 6: Marvel

1. I. Lilias Trotter, *A Way of Seeing: The Inward and Outward Vision of Lilias Trotter*, ed. and comp. Miriam Huffman Rockness (Mount Dora, FL: Lilias Trotter Legacy, Inc., 2020), 46, 80, 64, 14.
2. Ibid., dedication page.
3. "Lexicon: Strong's G2657 *katanoeō*," Blue Letter Bible, accessed April 6, 2022, https://www.blueletterbible.org/lexicon/g2657/kjv/tr/0-1/.
4. C. H. Spurgeon, *CSB Spurgeon Study Bible* (Nashville: Holman Bible Publishers, 2017), 1395.

Chapter 7: Believe

1. Brothers Grimm, *Hans in Luck*, narrated by Glenn Hascall, audiobook, Spoken Realms Publisher, 2014.
2. Ibid.
3. Ibid.

Chapter 8: Grieve

1. "Lexicon: Strong's G1690 *embrimaomai*," Blue Letter Bible, accessed April 6, 2022, https://www.blueletterbible.org/lexicon/g1690/kjv/tr/0-1/.
2. C. H. Spurgeon, "Jesus Wept," *Metropolitan Tabernacle Pulpit Volume 35*, June 23, 1889, https://www.spurgeon.org/resource-library/sermons/jesus-wept/#flipbook/.

Chapter 9: Trust

1. Samuel Rutherford, *The Loveliness of Christ: Selections from the Letters of Samuel Rutherford* (Moscow, ID: Community Christian Ministries, 2018), 55.

Chapter 10: Sorrow

1. Amy Carmichael, *Edges of His Ways* (Flintshire, UK: CLC Publications, 2020), 97, 230.
2. C. H. Spurgeon, *Cheque Book of the Bank of Faith* (Scotland: Christian Focus Publications, 1996), 331.

Chapter 11: Go

1. John Piper, *21 Servants of Sovereign Joy* (Wheaton, IL: Crossway, 2018), 557.
2. Charles H. Spurgeon, "Job Among the Ashes," *Metropolitan Tabernacle Pulpit Volume 34*, February 19, 1888, https://www.spurgeon.org/resource-library/sermons/job-among-the-ashes/#flipbook/.
3. Jeremiah Burroughs, *The Rare Jewel of Christian Contentment* (London: W. Bentley, 1651), 17.
4. Colleen Chao, "The Song I'll Sing Until My Last Day," *Revive Our Hearts* (blog), https://www.reviveourhearts.com/blog/the-song-ill-sing-until-my-last-day/.

Chapter 13: Confess

1. Thomas Watson, *All Things for Good* (Shawnee, KS: Gideon House Books, 2015), 21.

Chapter 14: Forgive

1. C. H. Spurgeon, "Forgiveness Made Easy," *Metropolitan Tabernacle Pulpit Volume 24*, https://www.spurgeon.org/resource-library/sermons/forgiveness-made-easy/#flipbook/.
2. Ibid.

Chapter 15: Let Go

1. Richard Sibbes, *The Bruised Reed* (Hillsville, VA: Evangelism Press, 2021), 126.
2. Ibid.

Chapter 17: Unravel

1. Alvin Tresselt, *The Mitten* (New York: HarperCollins, 1989), pages not numbered.
2. Susannah Spurgeon, *A Basket of Summer Fruit* (Forest, VA: Corner Pillar Press, 2010), 75–76.

Chapter 18: Ask

1. Colleen Chao, "The Gift of Cancer," *Revive Our Hearts* (blog), January 22, 2019, https://www.reviveourhearts.com/blog/true-hope-tuesday-gift-cancer/.
2. F. B. Meyer, *Jeremiah: Priest and Prophet* (New York: Revell, 1894), 176.
3. I. Lilias Trotter, *Parables of the Cross* (n.p.: First Start Publishing, 2012), 12.

Chapter 19: Rest

1. Paul Schlehlein, *John G. Paton: Missionary to the Cannibals of the South Seas* (Edinburgh: Banner of Truth Trust, 2017), xvii.
2. Ibid., 34–35.

Chapter 20: Step

1. Faith Cook, "Richard Baxter," *Singing in the Fire: Christians in Adversity* (Edinburgh: Banner of Truth Trust, 1995), 76.
2. Ibid., 77.

Chapter 21: Compare

1. Elisabeth Elliot, *Keep a Quiet Heart* (Ada, MI: Revell, 2004), 19–20.

Chapter 22: Want

1. Elisabeth Elliot, *Suffering Is Never for Nothing* (Nashville: B&H Publishing Group, 2019), 9.
2. Richard Sibbes, *A Breathing After God* (Minneapolis: Curiosmith Bookshop, 2018), 15.

3. Faith Cook, "Edward Payson," *Singing in the Fire: Christians in Adversity* (Edinburgh: The Banner of Truth Trust, 1995), 119.

4. Augustine, *The Confessions* (New York: Vintage Books, 1998), 218–19.

Chapter 23: Tell

1. Kate DiCamillo, *The Tale of Despereaux* (Somerville, MA: Candlewick, 2003), 79–81.

2. Colleen Chao, adapted from "Stories Are Light (in a Dark World)," Ethics and Religious Liberty Commission, August 17, 2016, https://erlc.com/resource-library/articles/stories-are-light-in-a-dark-world/.

Chapter 24: Lean

1. J. I. Packer, *Weakness Is the Way: Life with Christ Our Strength* (Wheaton, IL: Crossway, 2013), 15–16.

Chapter 25: Listen

1. Robert Hawker, *Piercing Heaven: Prayers of the Puritans*, ed. and comp. Robert Elmer (Bellingham, WA: Lexham Press, 2019), 48.

Chapter 26: Number

1. Lemuel Haynes, *May We Meet in the Heavenly World: The Piety of Lemuel Haynes*, ed. Thabiti M. Anyabwile (Grand Rapids, MI: Reformation Heritage Books, 2009), 2–14.

2. Ibid., 85–86, 88–89.

Chapter 27: Hope

1. "Lexicon: Strong's H8615 *tiqvâ*," Blue Letter Bible, accessed April 6, 2022, https://www.blueletterbible.org/lexicon/h8615/kjv/wlc/0-1/.

Chapter 28: Dance

1. C. H. Spurgeon, *Cheque Book of the Bank of Faith* (Scotland: Christian Focus Publications, 1996), 241.

2. C. H. Spurgeon, *Morning and Evening,* "The Things Unseen," January 29 (Peabody, MA: Hendrickson Publishers Marketing, LLC, 1995).

3. Colleen Chao, "The Strong and Gentle King Sings Over Me," *Revive Our Hearts* (blog), October 11, 2021, https://www.reviveourhearts.com/blog/the-strong-and-gentle-king-sings-over-me/.

Chapter 29: Understand

1. C. S. Lewis, *The Great Divorce* (New York: HarperOne, 2000), 69.

Chapter 30: Anticipate

1. C. S. Lewis, *The Last Battle* (New York: Harper Trophy, 2000), 196.

Chapter 31: Love

1. Corrie ten Boom, *God Is My Hiding Place* (Ada, MI: Chosen Books, 2021), 260.

Epilogue: Imagine

1. Rev. 19:11–16; 1:12–16; 4:2–11; Isa. 6:1; Pss. 29:3–9; 50:12; John 14:1–3; Isa. 25:6; Rev. 21:3–5; Isa. 35:8–10.

31 Days of Thanksgiving

1. *The Valley of Vision: A Collection of Puritan Prayers and Devotions*, ed. Arthur Bennett (Edinburgh: The Banner of Truth Trust, 1975), 26.